MW00845130

QGIS Quick Start Guide

A beginner's guide to getting started with QGIS 3.4

Andrew Cutts

BIRMINGHAM - MUMBAI

QGIS Quick Start Guide

Copyright © 2019 Packt Publishing

All rights reserved. No part of this book may be reproduced, stored in a retrieval system, or transmitted in any form or by any means, without the prior written permission of the publisher, except in the case of brief quotations embedded in critical articles or reviews.

Every effort has been made in the preparation of this book to ensure the accuracy of the information presented. However, the information contained in this book is sold without warranty, either express or implied. Neither the author, nor Packt Publishing or its dealers and distributors, will be held liable for any damages caused or alleged to have been caused directly or indirectly by this book.

Packt Publishing has endeavored to provide trademark information about all of the companies and products mentioned in this book by the appropriate use of capitals. However, Packt Publishing cannot guarantee the accuracy of this information.

Commissioning Editor: Richa Tripathi
Acquisition Editor: Aditi Gour
Content Development Editor: Kirk Dsouza
Technical Editor: Suwarna Patil
Copy Editor: Safis Editing
Project Coordinator: Hardik Bhinde
Proofreader: Safis Editing
Indexer: Priyanka Dhadke
Graphics: Alishon Mendonsa
Production Coordinator: Shraddha Falebhai

First published: January 2019

Production reference: 1240119

Published by Packt Publishing Ltd.
Livery Place
35 Livery Street
Birmingham
B3 2PB, UK.

ISBN 978-1-78934-115-7

www.packtpub.com

"For Catherine and Elodie"

`mapt.io`

Mapt is an online digital library that gives you full access to over 5,000 books and videos, as well as industry leading tools to help you plan your personal development and advance your career. For more information, please visit our website.

Why subscribe?

- Spend less time learning and more time coding with practical eBooks and Videos from over 4,000 industry professionals

- Improve your learning with Skill Plans built especially for you

- Get a free eBook or video every month

- Mapt is fully searchable

- Copy and paste, print, and bookmark content

Packt.com

Did you know that Packt offers eBook versions of every book published, with PDF and ePub files available? You can upgrade to the eBook version at `www.packt.com` and as a print book customer, you are entitled to a discount on the eBook copy. Get in touch with us at `customercare@packtpub.com` for more details.

At `www.packt.com`, you can also read a collection of free technical articles, sign up for a range of free newsletters, and receive exclusive discounts and offers on Packt books and eBooks.

Contributors

About the author

Andrew Cutts holds a geography degree and a masters degree in GIS and has almost 20 years of experience in working with geospatial technology. He currently works as a freelance geospatial consultant. He has worked in local government, large multinational companies, and small and medium-sized enterprises. He has run a geospatial blog for almost 3 years and is a co-host of the #scenefromabove podcast. Andrew has spoken at events worldwide on GIS and Earth observation. He is a keen user of Python, especially for rapid prototyping for geospatial challenges. Currently, he is working with clients to maximize their investment with geospatial technology through direct consulting, training, and technical writing.

About the reviewer

Alexander Bruy is an open source advocate and developer working on the QGIS project. He also develops tools such as Photo2Shape and QConsolidate plugins for QGIS and various Processing providers. He has been working with QGIS since 2006, and is now an OSGeo charter member, QGIS core developer, and community voting member. He is also the author of *QGIS By Example*, published by Packt Publishing.

Alexander is currently a freelance GIS developer and works for various companies worldwide.

Packt is searching for authors like you

If you're interested in becoming an author for Packt, please visit `authors.packtpub.com` and apply today. We have worked with thousands of developers and tech professionals, just like you, to help them share their insight with the global tech community. You can make a general application, apply for a specific hot topic that we are recruiting an author for, or submit your own idea.

Table of Contents

Preface

QGIS is an user-friendly open source GIS. Lately, open source GIS and QGIS has been gaining a lot of popularity.

Who this book is for

This book is a quick-start guide to QGIS 3.4. It is for anyone who wants to learn how to use QGIS to analyze geospatial data and create rich mapping applications. This book assumes no previous knowledge or experience.

What this book covers

Chapter 1, *Getting Started with QGIS 3*, covers the introduction and installation of QGIS 3, including a brief discussion of different versions. We will then look at opening QGIS, the layout of the software, the menus, and the toolbars.

Chapter 2, *Loading Data*, is where we will download and open various types of GIS data. We will talk about the different types of data and we will work predominately with the GeoPackage format. We will mention the GeoTIFF (raster) and Shapefile (vector) formats as well. We will use existing data to interact with the canvas via zoom/pan/selection. Finally, we will talk about saving a project and look at projections.

Chapter 3, *Creating Data*, will have you create a GeoPackage and build a simple project around it. We will create vector data. We will look at editing tools, as well as snapping and correcting errors. We will look at the attribute table and how to populate it. Finally, we will load in raster data and discuss how to create raster data.

Chapter 4, *Styling Data*, we will style our GIS data. We will look at styling options (there are many) for both vector and raster data. We will look at the Layer Styling Panel in QGIS.

Chapter 5, *Creating Maps*, will involve using data from the previous chapters to create maps. We will look briefly at labeling and examine, in more detail, how to create better and more aesthetically pleasing maps. Finally, we will look at the Atlas function.

Chapter 6, *Spatial Processing*, will see you use data in a GeoPackage to analyze your data. This chapter will be an introduction to the processing toolbox. We will look at individual tools and we will look at spatial queries on the data.

Chapter 7, *Expanding QGIS 3*, looks at expanding QGIS. This will be focused on plugins, model builder, and a small amount of command-line work.

To get the most out of this book

Follow the order of the chapters where possible; it will help you gain the most out of this book.

Download the example code files

You can download the example code files for this book from your account at www.packt.com. If you purchased this book elsewhere, you can visit www.packt.com/support and register to have the files emailed directly to you.

You can download the code files by following these steps:

1. Log in or register at www.packt.com.
2. Select the **SUPPORT** tab.
3. Click on **Code Downloads & Errata**.
4. Enter the name of the book in the **Search** box and follow the onscreen instructions.

Once the file is downloaded, please make sure that you unzip or extract the folder using the latest version of:

- WinRAR/7-Zip for Windows
- Zipeg/iZip/UnRarX for Mac OS
- 7-Zip/PeaZip for Linux

The code bundle for the book is also hosted on GitHub at https://github.com/PacktPublishing/QGIS-Quick-Start-Guide. In case there's an update to the code, it will be updated on the existing GitHub repository.

We also have other code bundles from our rich catalog of books and videos available at https://github.com/PacktPublishing/. Check them out!

Download the color images

We also provide a PDF file that has color images of the screenshots/diagrams used in this book. You can download it here: `https://www.packtpub.com/sites/default/files/downloads/9781789341157_ColorImages.pdf`.

Conventions used

There are a number of text conventions used throughout this book.

`CodeInText`: Indicates code words in text, database table names, folder names, filenames, file extensions, pathnames, dummy URLs, user input, and Twitter handles. Here is an example: "Double-click on the `.exe` file and step through the following installation screens."

Any command-line input or output is written as follows:

```
Airport_layer =
iface.addVectorLayer('D:/QGIS_quickstart/qgis_sample_data/shapefiles/airpor
ts.shp','airports','ogr')
```

Bold: Indicates a new term, an important word, or words that you see onscreen. For example, words in menus or dialog boxes appear in the text like this. Here is an example: "Click on **Finish** to exit."

Warnings or important notes appear like this.

Tips and tricks appear like this.

Get in touch

Feedback from our readers is always welcome.

General feedback: If you have questions about any aspect of this book, mention the book title in the subject of your message and email us at `customercare@packtpub.com`.

Errata: Although we have taken every care to ensure the accuracy of our content, mistakes do happen. If you have found a mistake in this book, we would be grateful if you would report this to us. Please visit www.packt.com/submit-errata, selecting your book, clicking on the Errata Submission Form link, and entering the details.

Piracy: If you come across any illegal copies of our works in any form on the Internet, we would be grateful if you would provide us with the location address or website name. Please contact us at copyright@packt.com with a link to the material.

If you are interested in becoming an author: If there is a topic that you have expertise in and you are interested in either writing or contributing to a book, please visit authors.packtpub.com.

Reviews

Please leave a review. Once you have read and used this book, why not leave a review on the site that you purchased it from? Potential readers can then see and use your unbiased opinion to make purchase decisions, we at Packt can understand what you think about our products, and our authors can see your feedback on their book. Thank you!

For more information about Packt, please visit packt.com.

Getting Started with QGIS 3

QGIS is free and open source software. It is a **Geographical Information System** (**GIS**). QGIS enables users to create, manipulate, and visualize spatial data. Spatial data is data associated to a location or a place, commonly defined in terms of vector (points, lines, or polygons) or raster (bitmap) data. The QGIS project began in 2002 as a way of importing and viewing data from **PostGIS** (also open source software that adds geographic support to PostgreSQL) enabled database. QGIS is arguably now the leading open source GIS software package.

QGIS 3 was a significant update in the QGIS series. If you are familiar with the QGIS project, you can inspect the changes in the visual changelog available at this website: `https://www.qgis.org/en/site/forusers/visualchangelogs.html`. The processing framework was rewritten and has improved the performance significantly. Now, QGIS 3 provides users access to Python 3. This means many of the plugins, that make QGIS so powerful, have been updated to be compatible with the new API. At the time of writing, QGIS 3 had been out for almost a year. QGIS 3.4 was released in October, 2018. It is scheduled to become the first **Long Term Release** (**LTR**) of the QGIS 3 series in early 2019.

This book is a quick start guide to QGIS; it uses the LTR 3.4 release as its foundation. It is recommended that you use this version while working through this book. The book has been written in such a way that you should be able to apply the foundational knowledge gained to future releases. However, QGIS is actively developed software and subject to change.

Topics covered in this introductory chapter include the following:

- Installing QGIS
- Toolbars and GUI

Installing QGIS

QGIS runs on most operating systems. It is even possible to install it on a Raspberry Pi! This is one of the reasons for the success of QGIS: it is supported on multiple platforms. The QGIS project provides ready-to-use packages as well as instructions to build from source code at `http://download.qgis.org`. In this quick start guide, we will cover how to install QGIS on two systems: Windows and Ubuntu.

Installing on Windows

There are two ways of installing QGIS on the Windows OS. Directly download the `.exe` file from `http://download.qgis.org`, or download it via the **OSGeo4W** installer. OSGeo4W is a small program that allows you not only to download and install QGIS, but also other OSGeo tools. We recommend that you use this installer for QGIS. You can download the 32-bit or the 64-bit OSGeo4W installers from `http://osgeo4w.osgeo.org`, or, you can download directly from `http://download.osgeo.org/osgeo4w/osgeo4w-setup-x86.exe` or `http://download.osgeo.org/osgeo4w/osgeo4w-setup-x86_64.exe`. Download the version that matches your operating system and keep it. In the future, whenever you want to change or update your system, just run it again.

OSGeo4W installer

In this section, we will look at the advanced installer and express installer options (which will install the latest release) using OSGeo4W as the installer.

Latest release

Once you have downloaded the installer that matches your system, double-click on the
.exe file and step through the following installation screens. The simplest way, which
installs the latest release, is to select **Express Desktop Install**. This may not install QGIS 3.4.
If you wish to do this, then please see the following subsection, *Advanced installer*. The
express installation option is shown in the following screenshot:

OSGeo4W setup

Select the checkboxes next to **QGIS**, **GDAL**, and **GRASS GIS**. GDAL is used for reading and writing geospatial data and **GRASS GIS** is open source GIS software that can be used in combination with QGIS. This is shown in the following screenshot:

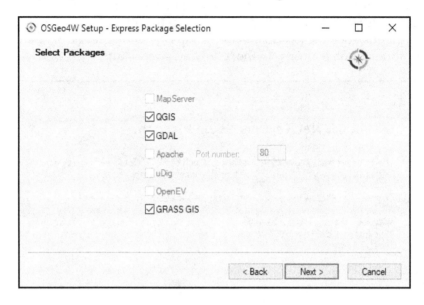

OSGeo4W setup, choosing options for install

Click **Next** and the downloading process will begin. Progress will be displayed as each component is downloaded and installed. Having these installed will provide you with many tools to perform geospatial analysis. After a short period of time, you should see OSGeo4W in your program menu, along with a subset of the software installed, including QGIS.

You can install multiple versions of QGIS. Sometimes, this may be necessary as plugins may not work with certain versions of the software. What if you want to choose a version? OSGeo4W allows this with the advanced installer.

Advanced installer

Run the OSGeo4W .exe file and select the radio button next to **Advanced Install**:

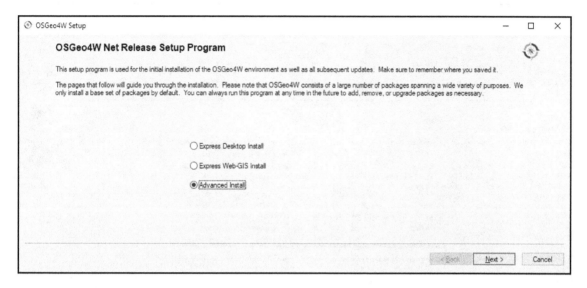

OSGeo4W setup (choosing Advanced Install)

Step through the installation wizard. When you get to **Select Packages**, choose the version you require. In the following screenshot, I have selected 3.4:

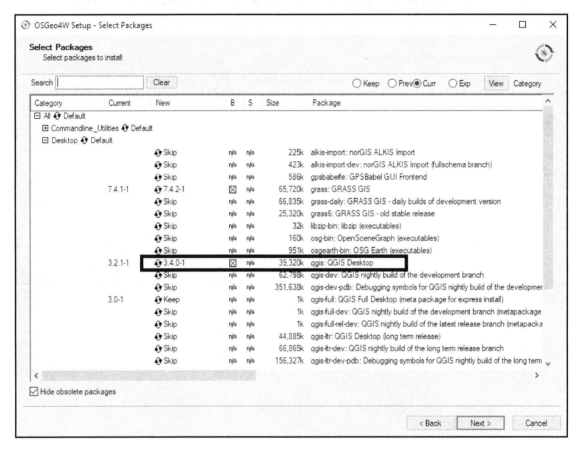

OSGeo4W setup (selecting packages to install)

You can select other packages if required. Once you have chosen the software, click on **Next** and the installation will begin.

Updating via OSGeo4W

You can use the OSGeo4W installer to install new updates. It will uninstall the previous version. You may have older versions installed on your system (perhaps installed with the standalone installer). To uninstall, locate the installation directory of the older version and run the `uninstall.exe` file. This is shown in the following screenshot:

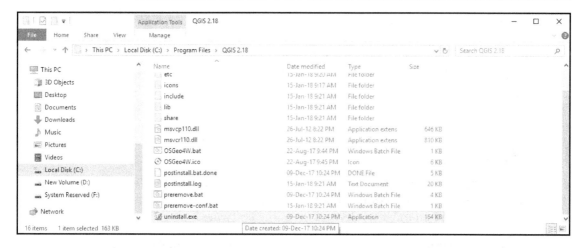

Windows Explorer

Step through the uninstallation wizard and, once uninstalled, you should get a similar message (depending on your version) to this:

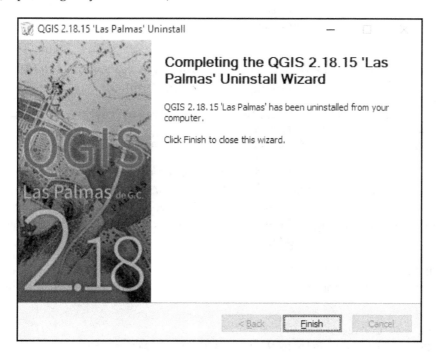

Uninstalling QGIS 2.18

Click on **Finish** to exit.

 It is possible to have multiple versions of QGIS running on your system.

Installing on Ubuntu

On Ubuntu, the QGIS project provides packages for the LTR, **Latest Release** (**LR**), and development versions (DEV). For this book, we recommend installing the LTR version. The LTR version is the current most stable version of the software.

To avoid conflicts that may occur due to incompatible packages, make sure that you only add one of the package source options. The specific lines that you have to add to the source list depend on your OS version. The following version is the latest release for Debian stretch:

```
deb      https://qgis.org/debian stretch main
deb-src https://qgis.org/debian stretch main
```

After choosing the repository, we will add the `qgis.org` repository's public key to our `apt` keyring. This will avoid the warnings that you might otherwise get when installing from a non-default repository. Run the following command in Terminal:

```
wget -O - https://qgis.org/downloads/qgis-2017.gpg.key | gpg --import
gpg --fingerprint CAEB3DC3BDF7FB45
gpg --export --armor CAEB3DC3BDF7FB45 | sudo apt-key add -
```

If necessary, you might need to make adjustments based on your system. For an updated list of supported Ubuntu versions, check out `http://www.qgis.org/en/site/forusers/alldownloads.html#debian-ubuntu`. By the time this book goes to print, the key information might have changed. Refer to `http://www.qgis.org/en/site/forusers/alldownloads.htm` for the latest updates.

Finally, to install QGIS, run the following commands. The first will fetch any updates to packages on your system; the second will install QGIS, the Python library, and the GRASS plugin:

```
sudo apt-get update
sudo apt-get install qgis python-qgis qgis-plugin-grass
```

This book has been written based on a QGIS installation on a Windows operating system. There may be slight visual changes between operating systems, especially the screenshots.

Using QGIS

Open QGIS from the installation location. If you followed the OSGeo4W installation on Windows, you should find it in under the `OSGeo4W Shell` folder in the Start menu. On loading, QGIS will appear similar to the following screenshot which I have annotated:

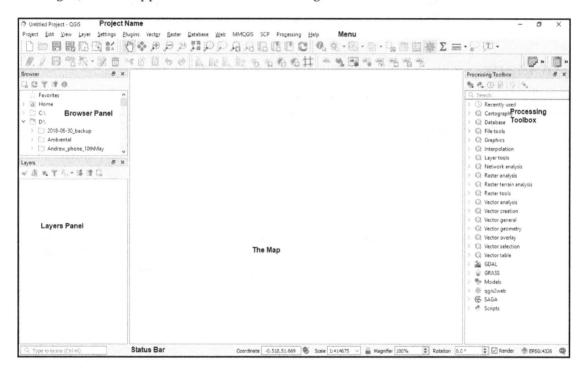

Overview of QGIS 3 annotated

The biggest area is reserved for the map.

Toolbar and panel overview

In this section, we will look at the panels and toolbars in QGIS and how to turn them on and off.

Panels

All panels are dockable; this means you can move them around as needed. To the left of the map, there are the **Layers** and **Browser** panels and to the right is **Processing Toolbox**. The **Browser** panel allows you find data in folders on your computer. From the **Browser** panel, you can drag data into the map. The **Layers** panel shows the data and its drawing order. Right-clicking on a layer in the **Layers** panel opens a context menu that lets you interact with that layer. We will be working with the **Layers** panel throughout this book. At the bottom of the QGIS project, we can see **Status Bar**. **Status Bar** is useful for quickly finding out what projection you are working in or the scale of the map. Finally, at the top of QGIS there is the window title (as yet unnamed project), menu options, and toolbars.

Toolbars

A toolbar is the place where tools are found! You can customize the toolbars to suit your work. These settings can be found via **Settings | Interface Customizaton**. In the previous screenshot, the toolbars were docked under the menu. Many of the tools can also be found via the menus as well. Hover the mouse cursor over a tool to find out more about it. It is also possible to build your own tools in QGIS using plugins.

Customizing

If you right-click near where I have annotated **Menu** in the previous screenshot, you can access **Panels** and **Toolbars**. If you accidentally turn a panel or toolbar off, then this is the place to turn it back on. You can also find these options via the **View** menu:

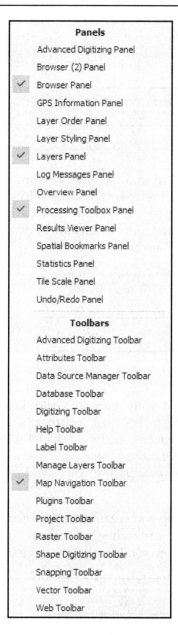

Panels

Advanced Digitizing Panel

Browser (2) Panel

✓ Browser Panel

GPS Information Panel

Layer Order Panel

Layer Styling Panel

✓ Layers Panel

Log Messages Panel

Overview Panel

✓ Processing Toolbox Panel

Results Viewer Panel

Spatial Bookmarks Panel

Statistics Panel

Tile Scale Panel

Undo/Redo Panel

Toolbars

Advanced Digitizing Toolbar

Attributes Toolbar

Data Source Manager Toolbar

Database Toolbar

Digitizing Toolbar

Help Toolbar

Label Toolbar

Manage Layers Toolbar

✓ Map Navigation Toolbar

Plugins Toolbar

Project Toolbar

Raster Toolbar

Shape Digitizing Toolbar

Snapping Toolbar

Vector Toolbar

Web Toolbar

Customizing the panels and toolbars

In the next section, we will briefly look at some of the main toolbars.

The main toolbars

The map navigation toolbar is shown in the following screenshot:

Map navigation toolbar

These tools are all about moving around the map. Panning (the hand icon), zooming (magnifying glass), creating a new canvas view (fourth icon from the right), and bookmarking locations (third and second icons from the right) are all part of this toolbar. These tools should be similar to any map-based application. You can also use the scroll wheel on your mouse to zoom in and out of your map.

The attribute toolbar is all about interacting with data. It is shown in the following screenshots:

Attribute toolbar

These tools allow you to identify the attributes of vector layers or values of raster layers (the blue i). Select and deselect features (third, fourth, and fifth icons from the left), then open the attribute table (the table icon), the field calculator (the abacus icon), measure tool (the ruler icon), and the text annotations button (the final icon on the bar). These tools are very commonly used and will become part of your standard interaction with GIS data in QGIS.

The project toolbar is about saving and creating new projects in QGIS. A project is what contains links to all your files, the order they are in, how they are styled, any print layout— basically everything about your project. It is shown in the following screenshot:

Project toolbar

These tools allow you to create a new project (paper icon), open a project (folder icon), save project and save project as (disk icons), create and manage print layouts (two icons), and finally use the style manager. We will look at the print layout in more detail in `Chapter 5`, *Creating Maps*.

If you click on **Project** from the menu bar, you will see the same icons appearing. This is generally true for all the menus and corresponding toolbars. It is sometimes easier to keep frequently used toolbars, such as editing toolbars, open, and keep the other ones that are not so frequently used hidden to save on screen space.

We will look at other toolbars in more detail as we progress through this book.

Summary

We have introduced QGIS 3 in this chapter. We looked at the options for installing on both Windows and Ubuntu. Finally, we had a quick look at the QGIS interface and the nomenclature of its features.

In the next chapter, we will look at loading data and interacting with it in QGIS. We will describe what GIS is and how to save a project.

2
Loading Data

The next two chapters are all about using data in QGIS. In Chapter 3, *Creating Data*, we will look at how we build and edit GIS data. In this chapter, we will start by loading existing data. QGIS supports many GIS data formats. It makes use of the OGR library for vector data and the GDAL library for raster data. By default, QGIS uses the GeoPackage format. As such, we will make this the default format for this book.

These are the topics that will be covered in this chapter:

- Vector, raster, and other data types
- GeoPackage
- Loading data
- Projections
- Creating and saving a project

GIS data

What do I mean by GIS data? By vector data, I mean points, lines, and polygons. The most common file format is a Shapefile (multiple files make up a Shapefile). By raster data, I mean (georeferenced) bitmaps. The most common file format is GeoTIFF.

Download the QGIS sample dataset from `https://github.com/PacktPublishing/QGIS-Quick-Start-Guide/blob/master/qgis_sample_data.zip`. Extract it to a working directory on your computer.

In QGIS, you should now be able to see this data in the **Browser** panel, as shown in the following screenshot:

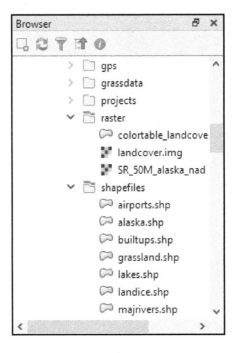

Browser panel

Loading data

Loading data into QGIS can be done in several ways. Three of the most common ways are as follows:

- You can drag data directly from a folder (Windows OS) straight into the map
- You can drag data from the **Browser** panel into the map

- You can click **Layer** | **Add Layer** and choose what type of layer to add to the map
- This way opens **Data Source Manager**

In the following screenshot, we are choosing to load **Add Vector Layer**, which can also be done using the *Ctrl + Shift + V* shortcut:

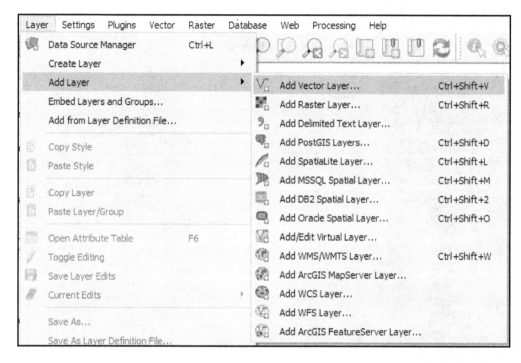

Loading data

This screenshot gives you an idea of all the different data types that QGIS can consume. We will not be covering all these formats; we mention it to highlight the data capabilities of QGIS only. By adding data this way, you will be opening **Data Source Manager**, as shown in the following screenshot:

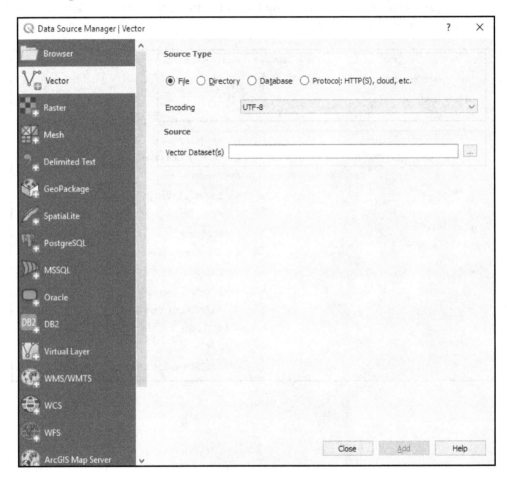

The QGIS Data Source Manager

Data Source Manager is a really nice way of adding data to your map. You can add files one by one, add multiple files, or add different file types at the same time. To use an analogy, **Data Source Manager** is very much like a data menu: just select the data you want.

From the QGIS sample data downloaded earlier, load `airport.shp` from the `shapefiles` folder and the `SR_50M_alaska_nad.tif` file from the `raster` folder. These should load into the map and appear as follows:

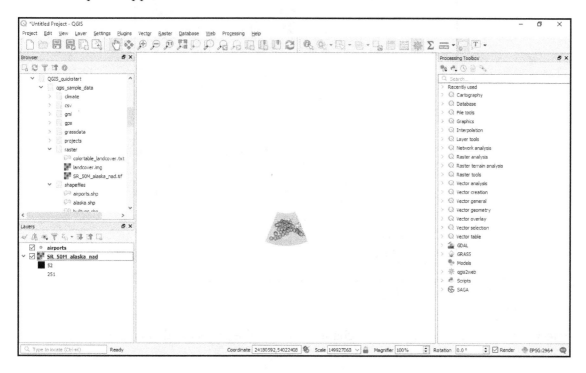

The overview of QGIS with data loaded

Right-click on SR_50M_alaska_nad and select **Zoom to Layer** to zoom to the layer extent. This is shown in the following screenshot:

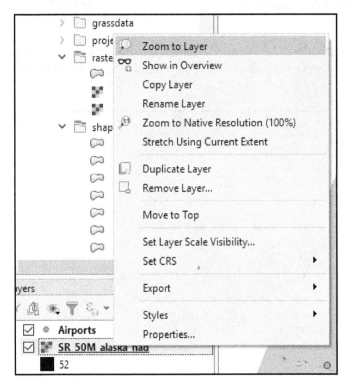

Zoom to Layer

Select **Project** | **New** and don't save changes to clear the project and open a new one.

GeoPackage

I have loaded all the Shapefiles in the shapefiles folder to a GeoPackage layer. You can download this layer from here: https://github.com/PacktPublishing/QGIS-Quick-Start-Guide/blob/master/Alaska_GeoPackage.zip.

Expand GeoPackage in the **Browser** panel, as shown in the following screenshot. In Chapter 3, *Creating Data*, we will look at how to add a layer to this package. For now, select the Airports layer and drag it into your map as follows:

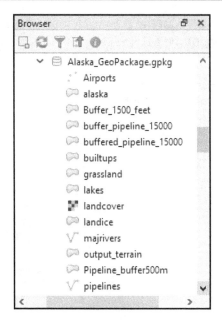

GeoPackage in the Browser panel

Experiment by dragging in more layers and zooming to the layer extent. This data looks no different to the Shapefiles we loaded previously. If you look at the file in your file manager (Windows Explorer, for example), instead of several Shapefiles and the several files associated to a Shapefile, we have one file. This makes the GeoPackage format (.gpkg) ideal for sharing and managing project data. The GeoPackage format has no file size limitations and is platform-independent, unlike a Shapefile.

Interacting with the data

In this section, we will use **Map Navigation** and **Attributes Toolbar**. Create a new project (**Project | New**) and load the following data from the GeoPackage into the QGIS project:

- Airports
- majrivers
- trees

Load `SR_50M_alaska_nad.tif` from the `raster` folder. Make sure the layers are ordered in this way. Zoom to the extent of the `Airports` layer. Your screen should look similar to the following screenshot:

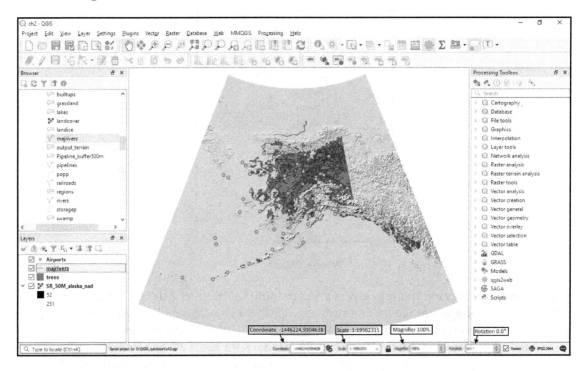

The overview of QGIS with layers added

Identifying data

From **Attributes Toolbar**, click on the blue i button and then click on a point from the `Airports` layer in the map. This will display the **Feature** attributes in a new panel; again, like all panels, you can move it around and resize as needed. The clicked point will be highlighted in the map and its attributes displayed, similar to the following screenshot:

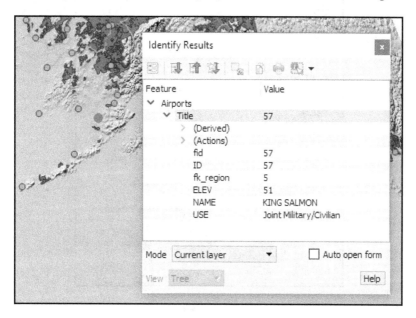

Identify tool

Investigate the identify tool with the other layers. Note that the **Mode** shown in the identify results is currently set to **Current layer**. That means that you only see the results from the layer that is currently active. There are four options in **Mode**:

- **Current layer**
- **Top down, stop at first**
- **Top down**
- **Selection**

Set **Mode** to **Selection** and click another location on the map. This time, you will be presented with identify options for all the layers (relating to the clicked location). This way, you get to choose the feature you wish to query. An example of this is shown in the following screenshot:

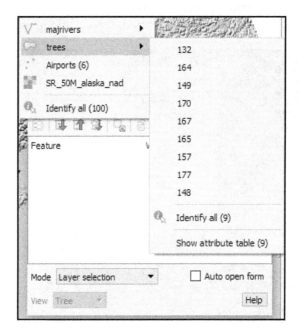

Identifying all layers

Close the identify results panel. Next, we will look at selecting data.

Data selection

There are several ways to select data in QGIS. In this chapter, we will look at the drawing selection options in **Attributes Toolbar** that we highlighted in Chapter 1, *Getting Started with QGIS 3*. Let's select some data from Airports. Click on the Airports layer in the **Layers** panel (making sure it is highlighted) and select the Select Features by area or single click button. Note that there are other ways of drawing a selection from the drop-down button, including selecting by polygon, freehand, and radius. In this example, we will use the default select features option, as shown in the following screenshot:

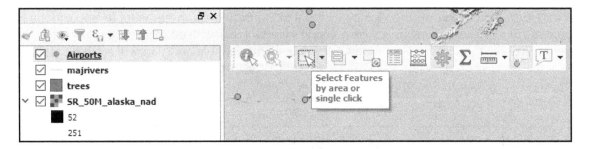

Select features by area or with a single click

Click and drag a box around several Airports' points. The selected points will change color. Press *F6* or click on the open table button in the toolbar. The attribute table for the `Airports` layer will appear. In the lower-left corner, set the query to **Show Selected Features**. This is shown in the following screenshot:

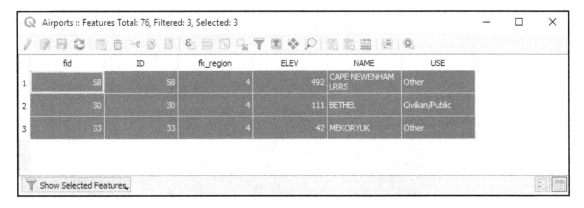

Attribute table for Airports layer

In the attribute table, click on the Invert selection (Ctrl+R) button (yellow right-angled triangle and clear triangle forming a square), as follows:

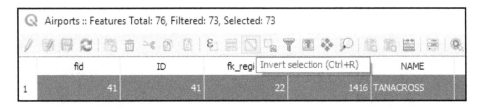

Inverting a selection

Inverting a data selection can often be useful. For example, you might want to select many points, but want to exclude only a few. Using inversion allows you to select the few and invert the selection to select the many. Close the attribute table and you will see the newly selected airports on the map. Click on Deselect Features from All
Layers from **Attributes Toolbar** to clear the selection. This is shown in the following screenshot:

Deselecting features from all layers

Finally, let's select a feature in the `Airports` layer by an attribute value. Click on the Select Features by Value button in **Attributes Toolbar**. This is shown in the following screenshot:

Selecting features by value

A selection dialog box will appear. Set the **ID** field to equal 1. Click on the **Select features** button and the selected airport will be highlighted in the map. You can click on **Flash features** to flash the selected airport and also click on **Zoom to features** to zoom into the selected airport.

The **Select Features by Value** dialog box is shown in the following screenshot:

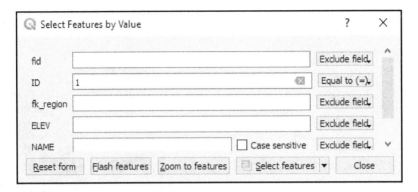

Select Features by Value dialog box

Click on the **Close** button and clear the selection (using the **Clear Selection** button shown previously). Note here that **Select Features by Expression** is also available. We will look at expressions in more detail later this book.

Measuring distance and area

A common function of a GIS is to quickly calculate distance and area. In Chapter 3, *Creating Data*, we will show how to write the area of a feature to an attribute table. In this chapter, though, we will look at the measuring options available from **Attributes Toolbar**.

The measure tool does not require a layer to be selected in the layer panel in order for it to work. This means that it is independent of layers. The measure tool can measure length, area, or angle, and you can use the drop-down button next to the tool to select the required option. In this example, let's measure length. Select the **Measure Line** option and then left-click on the map to begin the measurement. After doing this, left-click again to measure the segment. Continue to left-click to measure segments of the line or right-click on the end point to finish measuring.

The following screenshot shows the distance in meters between airports:

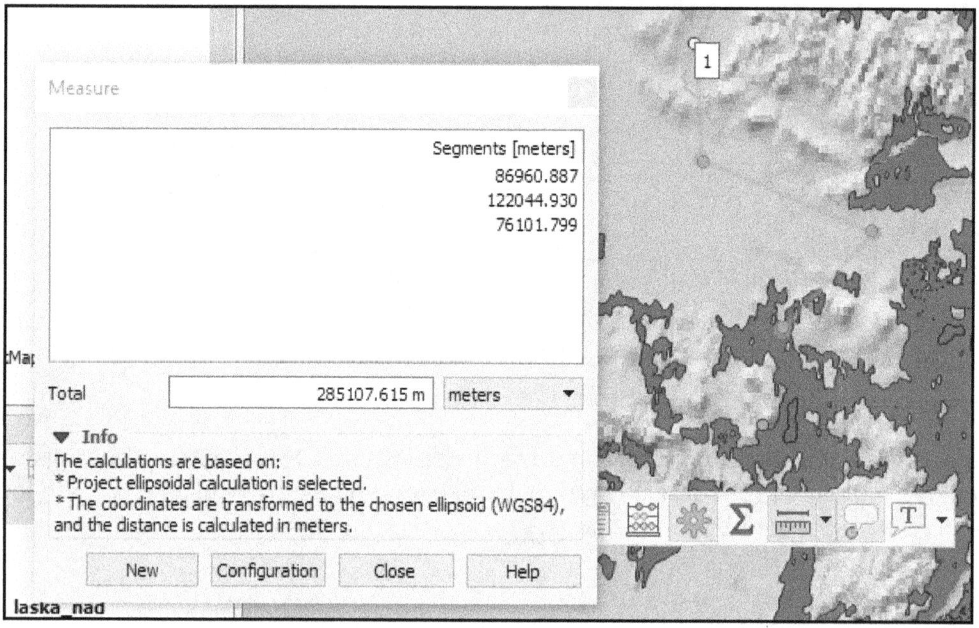

The Measure tool in QGIS

Change the units from **meters** to **kilometers** to show more meaningful distance at this scale. Try measuring area; the tool works in the same way as distance. Measuring in any GIS depends on the projection of the map. In the next section, we will look at projections in QGIS.

Projections

The default projection for QGIS (on loading the first time) has the EPSG code 4326 (WGS 84). Unless changed, the default settings in QGIS allow the projection of the map to be set by the projection of the first layer loaded into the map, assuming that the data has a projection associated to it.

It is beyond the scope of this book to go into details about various coordinate systems; if you are interested in learning more about this, then a good starting point is the Wikipedia entry on geographic coordinate systems at `https://en.wikipedia.org/wiki/Geographic_coordinate_system`.

Suffice to say that getting the projection correct in your GIS is fundamental to any analysis, mapping, or derivation of knowledge from your data. The world is not flat and projecting your data is the process of taking the part of the Earth's surface you are working on and mathematically shrinking and distorting it so it fits on a plane. You can move from one projection system to another by transforming your data.

Using the `Airports` layer as an example, the projection of the layer is EPSG 2964 and on loading the data, your QGIS project will be set to this projection. If you add data in another projection, then QGIS will make reprojections of your data on the fly. This is very powerful and useful, but be careful that you know what projection system all your data is in.

To illustrate projections, consider changing the projection from EPSG 2964 to EPSG 4326 with the internal reprojection parameters. Here is our data in the EPSG 2964 projection:

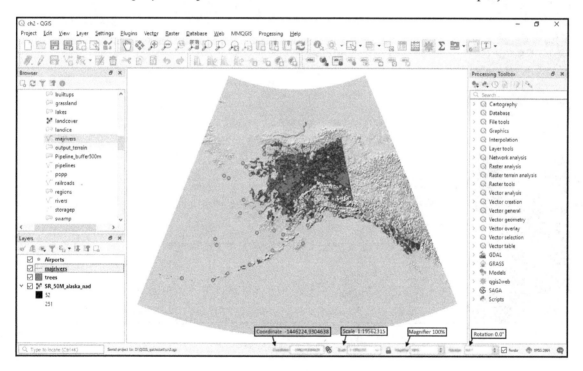

The overview of QGIS project in EPSG 2964

In the **Status Bar**, in the lower-right-hand corner you will see EPSG 2964. Click on this and change the projection to **WGS 84**. Search for 4326 in the **Filter** box as follows:

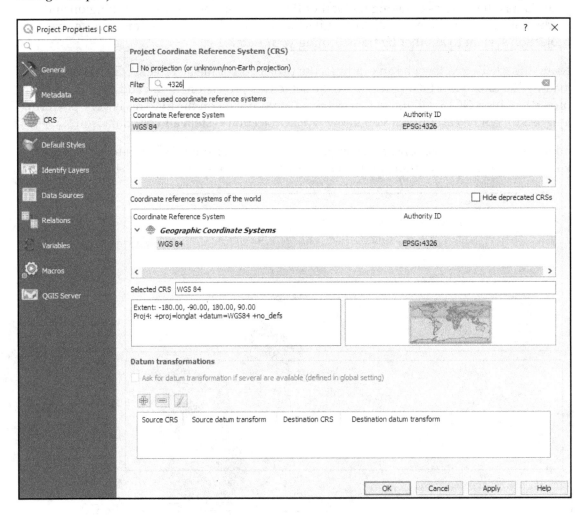

Overview of project projection properties

Click on **OK** and return to your map. You will see the data represented very differently to before. This is shown in the following screenshot:

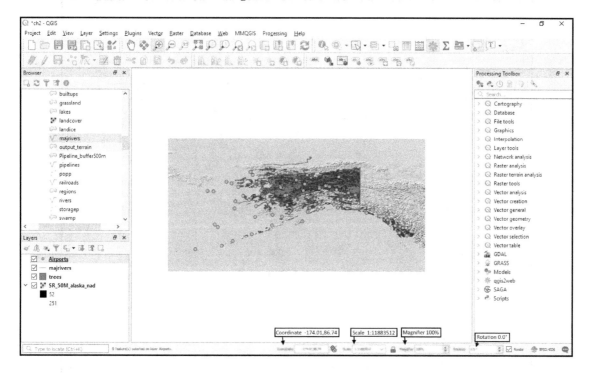

The overview of reprojected data

Reset the projection by repeating these steps and selecting EPSG 2964.

Saving data

In later chapters, when we start creating data, we will be working in one projection system. However, it is worth noting in this section that both vector data (points, line, and polygons) and raster data (bitmaps) can be saved in different projections. Right-click on the `Airports` layer and select **Export | Save Features As**. In the dialog box, you will see an option for **CRS**; this is where you can change the projection system.

This dialog box is shown in the following screenshot:

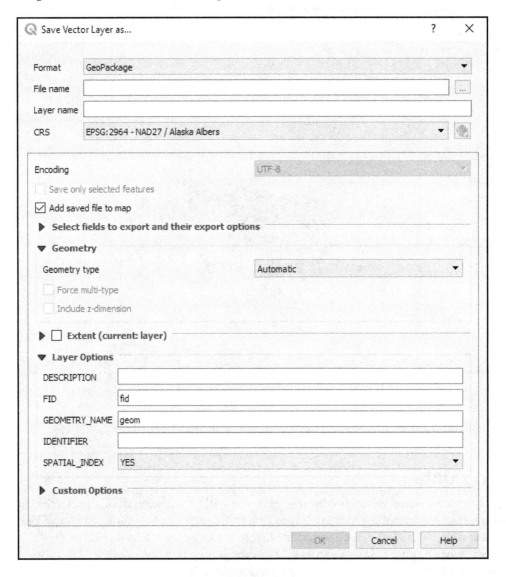

Saving the layer

For a raster, select **Raster** | **Projections** | **Warp (Reproject)** from the menu bar. This is shown in the following screenshot:

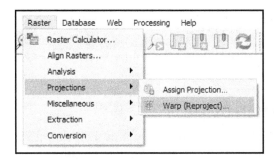

Reprojecting rasters in QGIS

The `Warp` command uses `gdalwarp` to reproject raster data. An example of reprojecting the `SR_50M_alaska_nad` raster to **EPSG:4326** is shown in the following screenshot:

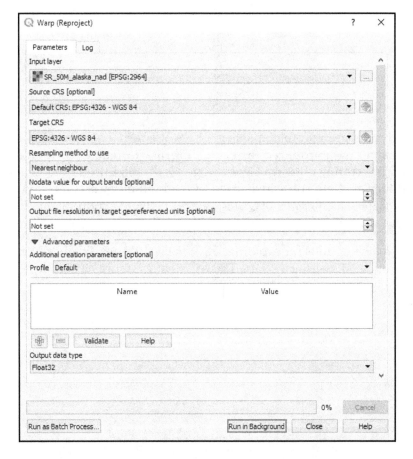

Reproject raster tool

If you scroll down to the bottom of this dialog box, you will see the corresponding `gdalwarp` command. This could be pasted into the OSGeo4W shell (if you installed QGIS via the OSGeo4W installer) and run on the command line (like so many QGIS functions).

Saving your project

We can save a QGIS project so we can return to it in the future. The default format is `.qgz`. To save your project, go to **Select Project** | **Save**. I have called mine `ch2.qgz`; it is shown in Windows Explorer as follows:

Saving the project as a .qgz file

Summary

We have looked at geographic/spatial data in QGIS. We talked about vector and raster formats. This chapter has introduced the default file new format, GeoPackage. In the next chapter, we will be creating data in a GeoPackage. QGIS still fully supports Shapefiles and GeoTIFFs, and they are both still widely used throughout many sectors and the GIS community. In Chapter 7, *Expanding QGIS 3*, we will look at exporting and loading text files into and out of QGIS.

We have explored the options for exploring data, via **Attributes Toolbar**. We looked at querying, selecting, and measuring data. There is so much more we can do, and in the next chapter we will look at building data in QGIS.

3
Creating Data

In this chapter, we will be creating GIS data. We will predominantly be working with GeoPackages. This is the default format for storing GIS data in QGIS 3.4. Instead of the many extensions that a Shapefile has, a GeoPackage can have hundreds of layers contained in one file, making it simpler to share and manage.

We will look at creating geometries of points, lines, and polygons. We will add attributes to a attribute table and use the Field Calculator to calculate the area of a polygon. We will briefly discuss the use of scratch layers and exporting our data to a Shapefile. Finally, we will look at how raster data is imported into a GeoPackage.

In this chapter, you will learn about the following topics:

- Creating a GeoPackage
- Creating vector data:
    - Editing geometry
    - Creating attributes
- Scratch layers and saving as a Shapefile
- Working with raster data in a GeoPackage

Creating data

As we noted in Chapter 1, *Getting Started with QGIS 3*, and Chapter 2, *Loading Data*, the default export GIS format in QGIS 3.4 is a GeoPackage. Any vector data operation that we perform can be applied to a Shapefile—at the end of this chapter, we will show how to export any vector layer in a GeoPackage into a Shapefile (you can also export to a number of other formats; see https://www.gdal.org/ogr_formats.html).

Open the QGIS project we created in `Chapter 2`, *Loading Data*. If you skipped the previous chapter, load the following layers from the GeoPackage associated with this book (available at this link): `https://github.com/PacktPublishing/QGIS-Quick-Start Guide/blob/master/Alaska_GeoPackage.zip`:

- `Airports`
- `majrivers`
- `trees`

Also load `SR_50M_alasja_nad.tif` from `QGIS_sample_data` (downloaded from `https://qgis.org/downloads/data/qgis_sample_data.zip`). Save this project as `Chapter3.qgz`.

Creating a GeoPackage

In this chapter, we will create some data. It will be captured in the same location and projection as the QGIS sample data. We will focus on mapping the island off the coast of Anchorage called **Fire Island**. First off, let's create a GeoPackage called `Fire_Island`.

To create a **New GeoPackage Layer** (a layer within a GeoPackage), we first need to create a new GeoPackage. From the **Layer** menu, select **Create Layer** | **New GeoPackage Layer**, as shown in the following screenshot:

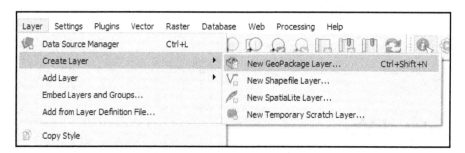

Creating a GeoPackage layer

In the resulting dialog box, fill in the parameters, as in the following screenshot:

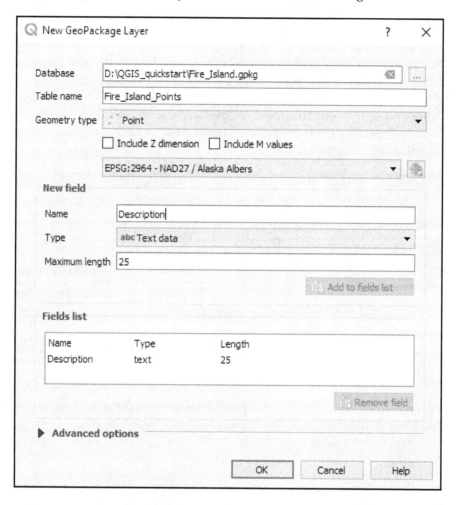

GeoPackage reference dialog box

We are going to create a layer in this GeoPackage called `Fire_Island_Points`, with **Geometry type** as **Point** and the coordinate reference system as EPSG 2964. Create a **New field** called `Description` and set its **Type** to **Text data** with a maximum **Length** of 25. Click on **Add to fields list** to add it to the field. We can always add extra fields later. Click on **OK**. When you click **OK**, a new GeoPackage will be created and the `Fire_Island_Points` layer will be added. You should have a new layer in the **Layers** panel called `Fire_Island_Points`. If you right-click on this layer and select **Open Attribute Table**, the associated table for this layer will appear. It will be empty and will have a **fid** field (assigned by default) and the **Description** field that we just created. This is shown in the following screenshot:

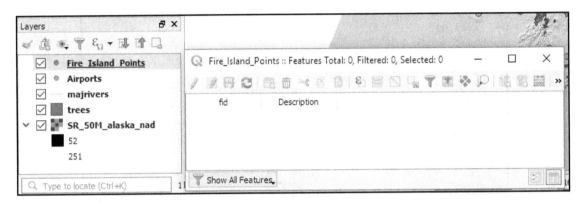

Layers and attribute table

We have now created a GeoPackage and a **Point** layer within that GeoPackage. We now need to create some data. Before we do that, we need to locate Fire Island to have something we can base our data on! Fortunately for us, QGIS makes this very easy as it allows you to add `OpenStreetMap` to your project.

In the **Browser** panel, find `XYZ Tiles` and expand it. Inside should be `OpenStreetMap`. Click and drag this into the map. It will appear as a new layer in the **Layers** panel. Adjust the order of the layers in the **Layers** panel to match those shown in the following screenshot:

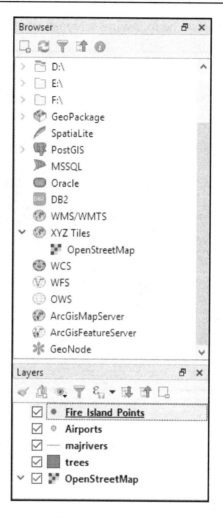

Browser panel and Layers panel

Navigate the map to find Anchorage, and you should see Fire Island. It is located off the coast to the west of Anchorage. At this point, turn off all the other layers except for `Fire_Island_Points` and the `OpenStreetMap` layer.

Your project should now look like the following screenshot:

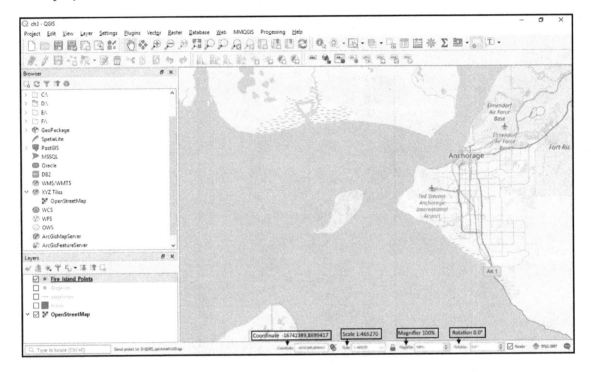

Overview of OpenStreetMap displayed in QGIS 3.4

In the next section, we will create some data using **Digitizing Toolbar**.

Digitizing data

In this section, we will create point, line, and polygon data in QGIS. We will create this data in the GeoPackage we have just created.

Creating points

Zoom into Fire Island so that the airport appears. We will now create a point to represent this airport. Make sure that **Digitizing Toolbar** is visible. You can turn it on by selecting **View** | **Toolbars** | **Digitizing Toolbar**. **Digitizing Toolbar** is shown in the following screenshot:

Digitizing Toolbar

Make sure that the `Fire_Island_Points` layer is selected in the **Layers** panel and click on the Toggle Editing button (yellow pencil) to start an editing session. The digitizing tools are now active in the toolbar, as shown in the following screenshot:

Digitizing tools with Toggle Editing activated

Click on the Add Point Feature button (three green dots). The mouse cursor will change to cross hairs. Click on the airport location in the `OpenStreetMap` data. A **Feature Attributes** dialog box will open. In here, accept **Autogenerate** for **fid** (this assigns a unique identifier to a feature), and for **Description**, type `Fire_Island_Airport`. This is shown in the following screenshot:

Fire_Island_Points feature attributes

A new point will be created. On the **Digitizing Toolbar**, click on save (the blue disk). Open the attribute table. You will see this newly added point. While still in editing mode, let's add a new field. With the attribute table opened, click on New field (Ctrl+W), as shown in the following screenshot:

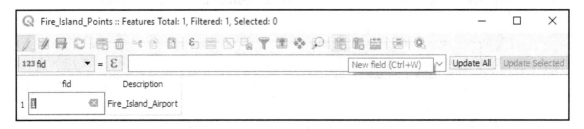

Attribute table

This will open a dialog box called **Add Field**. Create a new field called Type and set its **Length** to 25 (25 because we are not expecting any string entered to be greater than 25 characters). This is shown in the following screenshot:

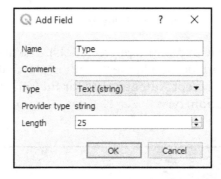

Adding a field

Click on **OK** and the newly created field will appear as a **NULL** value in the attribute table. Click on the **NULL** value and change it to Airport. In the attribute table, click on the save button and then the Toggle Editing button (yellow pencil) to stop editing. We have now created a point layer in a GeoPackage, added attributes, and created a new field. Let's use this knowledge to create a road layer (line) and an island outline layer (polygon).

Creating line data

From the **Layer** menu, select **Layer | Create Layer | New GeoPackage Layer**, as we did before. Fill in the dialog box to match the following screenshot:

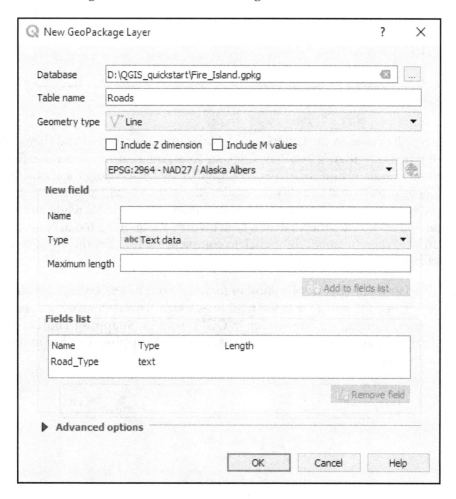

Creating a Roads layer

Click on **OK**. You will be prompted as to whether you wish to **Overwrite**, **Add new layer**, or **Cancel**. In this case, click on **Add new layer**, as shown in the following screenshot:

New GeoPackage layer message box

A `Roads` layer will appear in the **Layers** panel. Make sure it is selected and then click on Toggle Editing from **Digitizing Toolbar**. Click on Add Line Feature. This time, find an existing road on the island and digitize it. You digitize by left-clicking the mouse and then moving to a new location and left-clicking again—the software will join up these two clicks, known as **nodes or vertexes**. You can click on the zoom and pan tools while editing to zoom around and make the process easier. Don't worry about being too accurate, this is a learning exercise. When finished, right-click to complete the line. Set the `Road_Type` field to blacktop and click save.

Let's create another road. This will be another feature in our `Roads` layer. To maintain the topology, we will need to ensure that the road lines touch. This is done by snapping. We can snap to vertex, segment, or intersection in QGIS. Turn on **Snapping Toolbar** by clicking **View** | **Toolbars** | **Snapping Toolbar**. In an edit session, **Snapping Toolbar** looks as in the following screenshot:

Snapping Toolbar

In this case, the snapping tolerance has been changed to **10** pixels, but you can make adjustments to this based on your zoom level. This is not necessarily a one-size-fits-all, and you will need to adjust this parameter to suit your requirements. Set the snapping environment to **Vertex and Segment** to ensure you have the chance to snap to an adjoining road, as shown in the following screenshot:

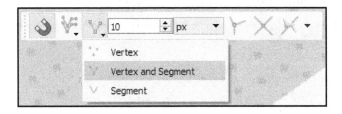

Snapping options

You are looking for a pink square to appear inside your cross hair digitizing cursor. You may need to zoom in. It will look as in the following screenshot:

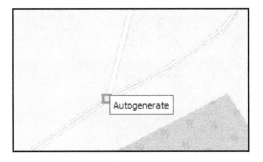

Snapping at the point

Create a new road and use snapping to ensure that the lines are topologically correct—that is, have no gaps. When you have finished digitizing, right-click and add blacktop in the Road_Type field and click save. Click Toggle Editing to finish the digitizing. You can continue to digitize more roads if you wish.

Creating polygons

Finally, in this vector editing section, we will take a look at editing polygons. All the techniques we have learned for lines and points apply. Again, create a new layer in your GeoPackage, and this time call it `Island_Outline`. We are not going to be creating any fields, so accept the defaults shown in the following screenshot:

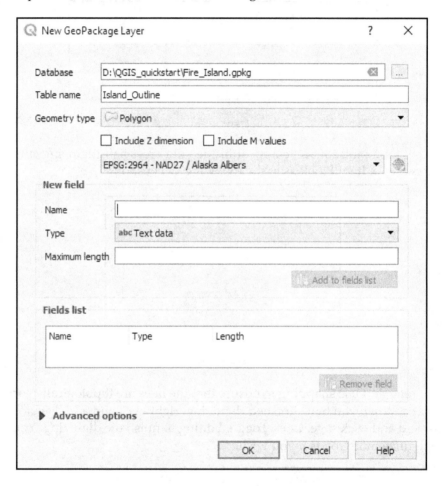

Creating a polygon Layer

Select the new layer in the **Layers** panel, click Toggle Editing and digitize the island. Don't worry about being too detailed. The result will be a digitized island. In QGIS, the new polygon layer will appear similar to the following screenshot:

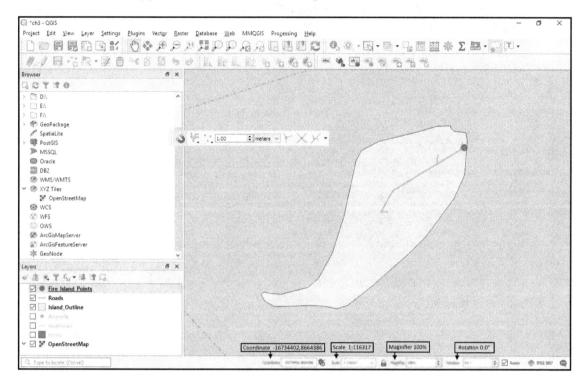

Overview of editing inside QGIS

Now let's create a field called `area` and populate its actual area. To do this, we will use the **Field Calculator** tool in **Attributes Toolbar**. With `Island_Outline` selected, click on the **Field Calculator** button (the abacus icon). Enter the following values: **Create a new field** called `area`, set it as **Whole number**, and in the **Expression** box enter `$area`. This is shown in the following screenshot:

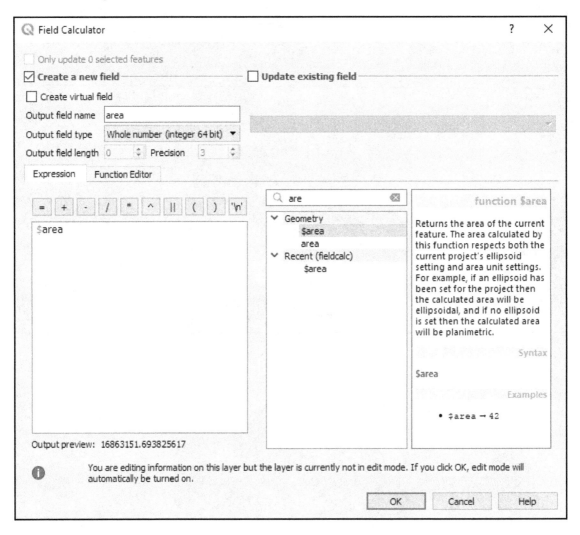

Field Calculator

Click on **OK**. This will turn on Toggle Editing, create a new field called `area`, and populate it with the area. If you have multiple features, all the areas will be calculated. Or, you can select the features you want to calculate the area for by using the selection tools. The Field Calculator tool is a flexible and very powerful tool. The resulting area is shown in the attribute table. When calculating area remember all units will be calculated in the units of the projection. If you wanted to check the area, you could use the measure tool shown in `Chapter 2`, *Loading Data*, to verify this measurement. Untoggle the edit session and save the project.

Scratch layers

Scratch layers are temporary vector layers that remain present while the QGIS project you are working on is open, but are lost upon closing—they are stored in memory. Scratch layers are useful when you want to quickly draw some features on a map. The benefit is that you don't need to think about file formats and locations for your temporary data. If you find you need to keep the layer, it can be exported as a permanent file—we will look at this in the next section.

To create a scratch layer, select **Layer** | **Create Layer** | **New Temporary Scratch Layer**. Select **Polygon / CurvePolygon** as **Geometry type**, as shown in the following screenshot:

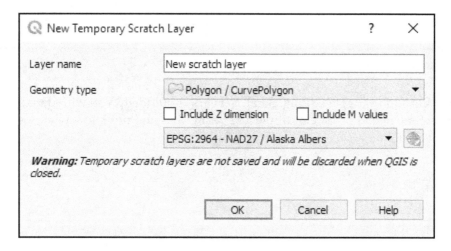

Creating a scratch layer

Digitize around one of the water bodies on `Fire_Island` using the techniques we have already highlighted. Your project will look like the following screenshot:

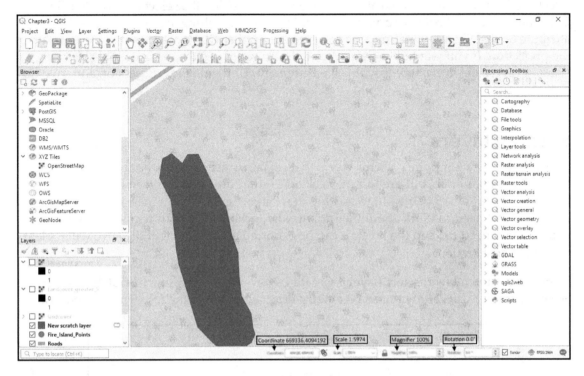

Overview of Digitized water body

Save your edits and untoggle editing. Scratch layers should help you with data management—no need to create multiple `test.shp` files and not know what they are any more.

Saving data to Shapefiles

We might want to save this scratch layer to a Shapefile. In fact, we can follow the same method for saving any of our data to a Shapefile. Right-click on the layer and select **Export | Save Features as**. From the drop-down menu next to **Format**, choose **ESRI Shapefile**, as shown in the following screenshot:

Saving to a Shapefile

Accept the defaults and a new Shapefile will be created.

Raster data

For the main, raster data that you create will be created via processing tools such as interpolation or the gridding of point data. Sometimes, we may want to rasterize a vector layer. This can be done using the **Raster | Conversion | Rasterize** command.

Let's load the `SR_50M_alasak_nad.tif` raster into the GeoPackage we have just created. You can just drag the layer in the **Browser** panel into the GeoPackage. It will show a message box once loaded, as in the following screenshot:

Importing a Raster layer to a GeoPackage

The `Fire_Island.gpkg` GeoPackage will now look like the following screenshot:

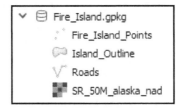

Contents of the GeoPackage

It is that simple to add data to a GeoPackage. Drag this layer into the map to check that it is actually present.

Creating a raster dataset

We are going to perform a query on the `landcover` data to create a new layer and then move it into the `Fire_Island` GeoPackage. Load the `landcover` raster from the `raster` folder in the QGIS sample data into the **Layers** panel.

Next, select **Raster | Raster Calculator** from the main menu. Fill in **Raster Calculator**, as shown in the following screenshot:

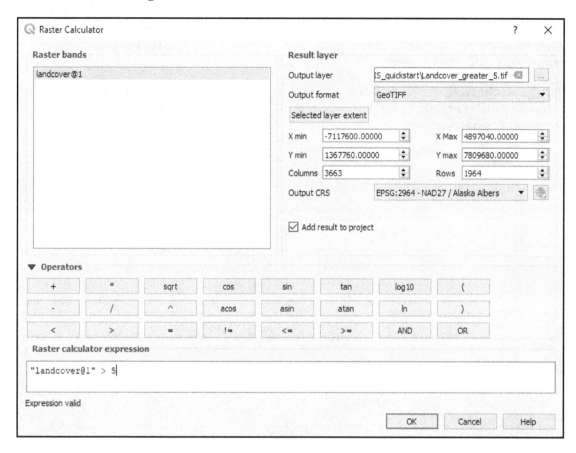

Raster Calculator

Save the new raster to a GeoTIFF file and click on **OK**. This will create a mask—anything with a `landcover` value greater than five will be assigned a value of one, and everything less than five will be assigned a value of zero. In the next chapter, we will show how we can display this data in a more meaningful way, setting transparency and changing color ramps.

Finally, drag this newly created layer into the `Fire_Island` GeoPackage.

Summary

We have looked at creating vector and raster data. Using the default GeoPackage format in QGIS is a powerful, yet simple, way to manage our GIS data. In this chapter, we have built geometries for points, lines, and polygons, and assigned attributes. We have created scratch layers, Shapefiles, and rasters.

In the next chapter, we will look at this attribute data to style our data. We will use the values in a raster to utilize different color ramps. The next chapter is a stepping stone on our way to creating a map, which we will do in Chapter 5, *Creating Maps*.

4
Styling Data

In this chapter, we will be styling GIS data. We will be using data stored in a GeoPackage. We will style vector layers based on data in the attribute table, and raster data using the vast array of rendering tools available to us. After we have created the styles, you can save and reuse them.

QGIS, by default, will randomly assign colors to every layer, and while this was useful when editing and creating, we'd like to visualize our data better. This will help us to produce a much more useful and pleasing map. This is the focus of this chapter.

These are the topics covered in this chapter:

- Layer Styling Panel
- Styling vector data
- Styling raster data
- Saving style files

Layer Styling Panel

The **Layer Styling** Panel offers a shortcut to the styling options of the **Layer Properties** dialog box. It allows the user to make updates to the styling of a layer and see it update instantly on the map.

Open QGIS. Load the following layers from the GeoPackage, and keep them in the following order in the **Layers** panel:

- `Airports`
- `majrivers`
- `grassland`
- `alaska`

The layers are ordered from the top in points, lines, and polygons for ease of visibility. Turn on the **Layer Styling Panel**. Do this by clicking on **View** I **Panels** I **Layer Styling Panel**, as shown in the following screenshot:

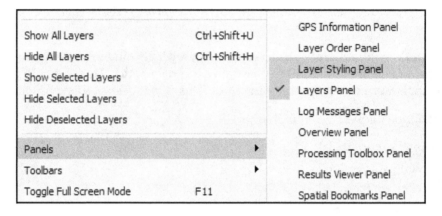

Activating the Layer Styling Panel

Once you turn on the Layer Styling Panel make sure that the checkbox next to **Live update** (bottom right of the Panel) is ticked so any updates can be seen as they are made.

Right-click on the `alaska` layer and select the **Zoom to Layer** option. Your screen should look similar to the following screenshot:

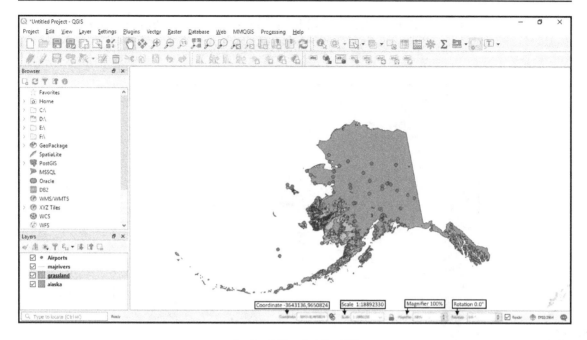

Overview of all layers loaded into QGIS

Styling vector data

In this section, we will explore the options for styling vector data. We will look at clustering point data and converting it to a heatmap. We will look at styling the major rivers in Alaska, but first we will explore the options for styling polygon data, beginning with the boundary of Alaska.

Styling polygon data

In this section, we will be styling the `alaska` and `grassland` layers. Turn all the other layers off in the **Layers** panel. We will style the data via the **Layer Styling** Panel on the right in the preceding image, as it is interactive. However, if you prefer, you can access the same information by right-clicking on a layer and selecting **Properties** and then **Symbology** tab.

Choose **Single symbol** and from the symbol layer, type then select **Shapeburst fill**. **Shapeburst fill** is the shading of the interior edge of a polygon. I have chosen a blue color for the border of my `alaska` layer. Set the distance of the fill to **2.00** millimeters as follows:

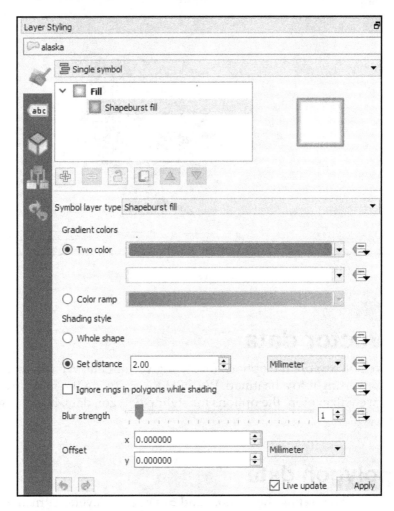

Layer Styling Panel

This produces a nice styling. We can refine it even further. Click on the checkbox next to **Ignore rings in polygons while shading**. Then, click on the **Draw effects** button and select the customize effects button. From the resultant dialog box, set the effect to **Colorise** as shown in the following screenshot:

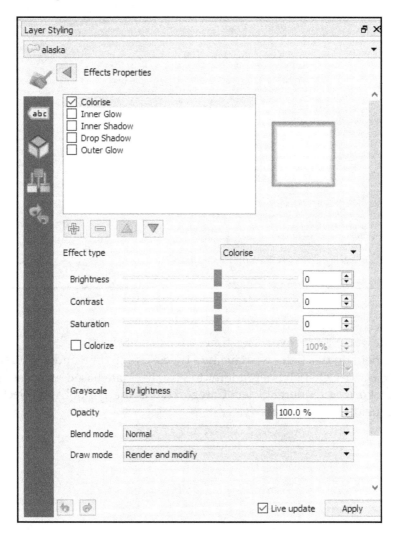

Advanced polygon styling in the Layer Styling Panel

The `alaska` layer should now be styled and look similar to the following screenshot:

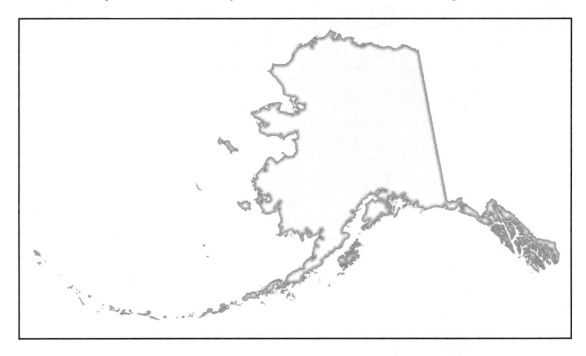

Alaska boundary styled

Next, turn on the `grassland` layer. This time, we will style it using the **F_CODEDESC** field. In this field, we have two types: `grassland` and `Scrub/Bush`. This data is split into classes. QGIS has a renderer to visualize data based on a class in a field; it is called the **Categorized** renderer. Select **Categorized** as the symbol and select the **F_CODEDESC** field. Click on **Classify**.

Next, double-click on `grassland` and set that to the **wine** symbol, as shown in the following screenshot:

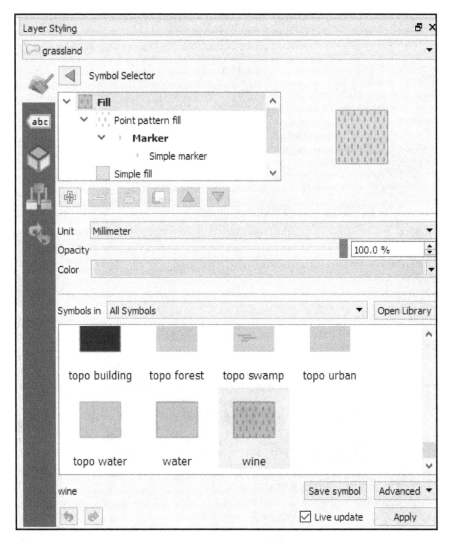

Symbolizing the grassland

Return to the original style selection window by clicking the blue triangle next to the **Symbol Selector** label. Double-click on grassland and change the symbol to **dotted**, as shown in the following screenshot:

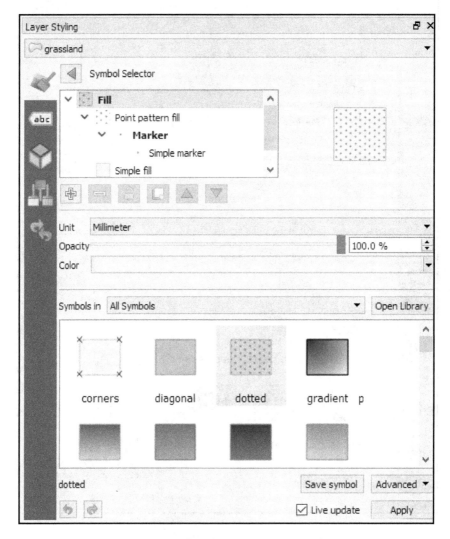

Symbolizing grassland (2)

Your data should now look similar to the following screenshot:

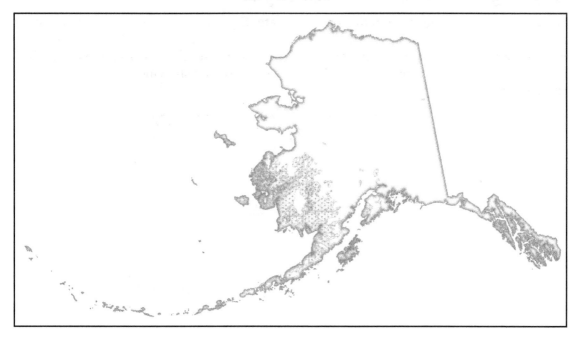

Alaska with the grassland symbolized

There are many ways we can style polygon data. Explore the options in the styling menu which can help tune up your visualization if needed. Next, we will take a look at line styling using the `majrivers` layer in our GeoPackage.

Styling line data – rivers layer

Select the `majrivers` layer from the top of the **Later Styling** panel. We will use this layer to create a **Line** style that consists of two colors: a fill color and an outline color. Select a **Single symbol** in the **Layer Styling** Panel. Beneath this **Symbology**, click on the green plus icon to add a new simple line. You should now have two lines showing, which will look similar to the following:

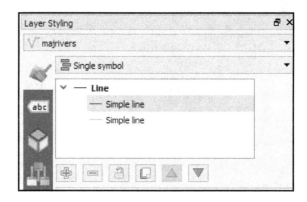

Styling the river as lines

Change the top simple line to a blue color of thickness 0.260000 and the bottom to a gray/black color of thickness 0.460000. Click on **Line** (directly above these two lines) to highlight the symbol. This will change the **Layer Styling** Panel slightly. At the bottom of this panel, there is a button labeled advanced. Click on this and select symbol levels. From the resultant screen, select the **Enable Symbol Levels** checkbox. Your data should now look similar to the following screenshot:

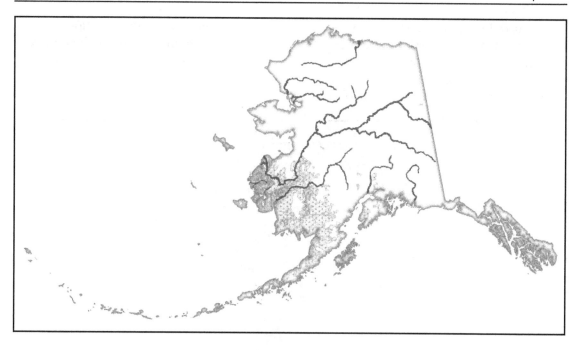

Alaska with the major rivers symbolized

Next, we will look at styling the `Airports` layer.

Styling points – Airports layer

There are many options involving in styling points. First, let's have a look at some of the options.

Point clustering option styles a point layer by clustering point features that are close to other point features. It assigns a number style to the clustered point to indicate the number of points clustered. Turn the `Airports` layer on and, in the **Layer Styling** Panel, select point clustering. Accept the defaults. You should now have a red marker with the number of points (clusters) at that location. Your map should look similar to this:

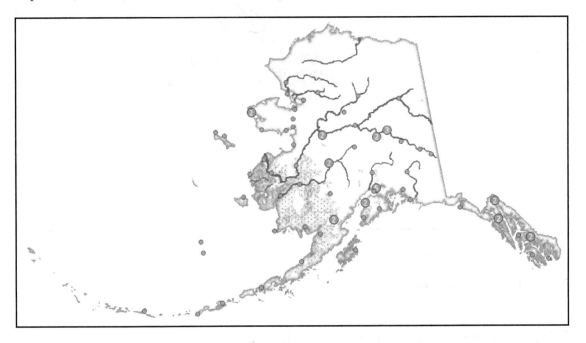

Alaska with the airports data displayed as a cluster

Heatmap creation is another option for points. Similar to clustering, we can create density heatmaps of the points on the fly. From the drop-down list, this time select **Heatmap**. Choose a suitable **Color ramp**; in the following example, I have chosen the **Spectral** color ramp. The point data associated with the `Airports` dataset is fairly sparse, and, really heatmap here doesn't serve much purpose for visualizing the data. However, it is a useful tool to know about:

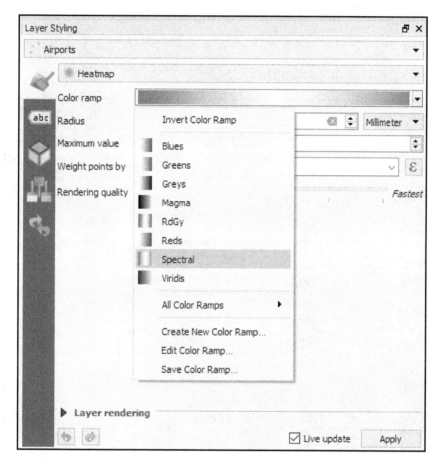

Creating a heatmap from point data

A better way would be to display the airport locations not as heatmaps or as point clusters, but as airplane symbols. Use the **Categorized** option for **Symbology** in the **Layer Styling** Panel. Select **USE** as **Column** that will define whether the airport is for the following:

- **Civilian/Public**
- **Joint Military/Civilian**
- **Military**
- **Other**

This is shown in the following screenshot:

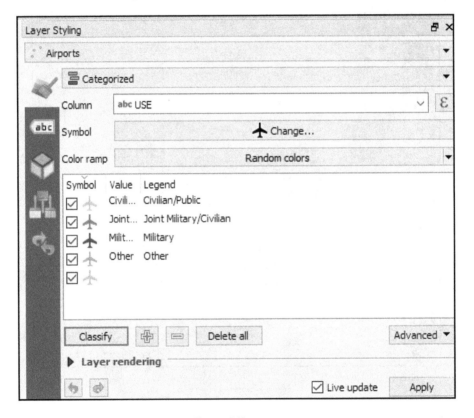

Airports styled by category

By displaying the data in this way, it is possible to see that the majority of the airports are classified as other. This helps us style the map better. This way, we can turn on/off using the check boxes for the airports we wish to display. If we only want to display civilian airports, we can uncheck all the other airport types. The resultant map will look like the following:

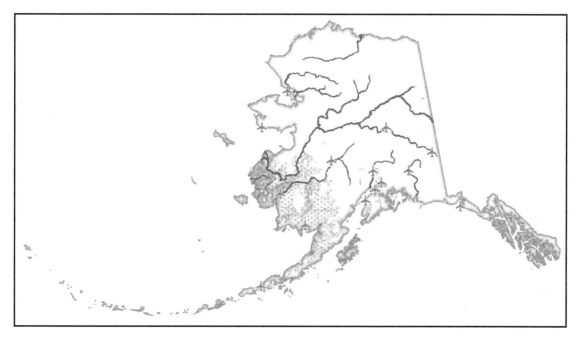

Alaska with the civilian airport data displayed

A word on data management

It is possible to achieve the same result as shown in the previous section by querying the data directly to only show a selection of data. We could duplicate the same layer, query it, and symbolize it differently, without having any impact on the underlying data. To duplicate the airport data, right-click on the layer in the layer panel and select duplicate layer. This will add exactly the same layer again to the map. You can change **Symbology** now, or add labels (more in `Chapter 5`, *Creating Maps*).

Right-click on the new layer and select filter. You can use **Query Builder** to build a query that selects only the **Military** airports. Double-click **USE** from **Fields**, then select **=** from **Operators**, and finally click on **All** in **Values** and select **Military**. **Query Builder** will look like the following screenshot:

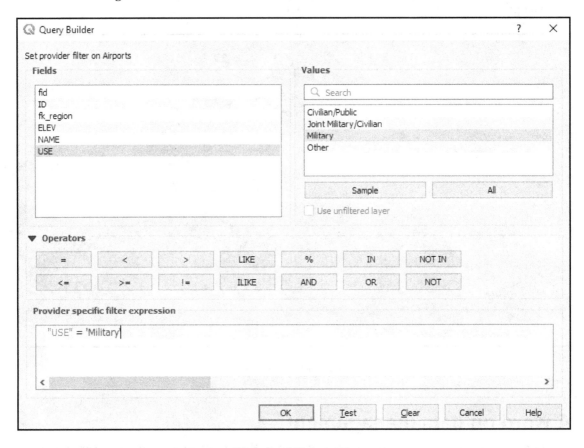

Using the Query Builder to select data

Click on **OK**, and then click **OK** again to exit the properties dialog box. Now, on the map only military airports will be displayed. This filtering is another way of working with your data. If you open the attribute table for this layer only, only the filter features will be displayed.

Styling raster data

Turn off all the vector layers. In this section, we are going to focus on rendering raster data. Load into the map the SR_50M_alaska_nad and landcover layers. We will style these layers. The options for styling raster data include the following:

- **Multiband color**: When you have three or more raster bands (for example, a satellite image), this option allows you to choose which bands are for the red, green, and blue channels
- **Paletted/Unique values**: Colors discrete raster data (landcover classification, for example)
- **Singleband gray**: Applies a black to white or white to black color ramp for continuous raster data (elevation data, for example)
- **Singleband pseudocolor**: Will apply a color ramp to continuous raster data (elevation data, for example)
- **Hillshade**: Will style a DEM as a hillshade raster on the fly

The SR_50M_alaska_nad image will, by default, load as **Singleband gray**. In the **Layer Styling** Panel, change **Symbology** to **Singleband pseudocolor**. Expand **Min / max values settings** and select **Cumulative count cut** to 1% to 99%, keep **Interpolation** as **Linear** (as it is a continuous raster dataset), and choose **Viridis** as **Color ramp**.

The **Layer Styling** Panel should look similar to the following screenshot:

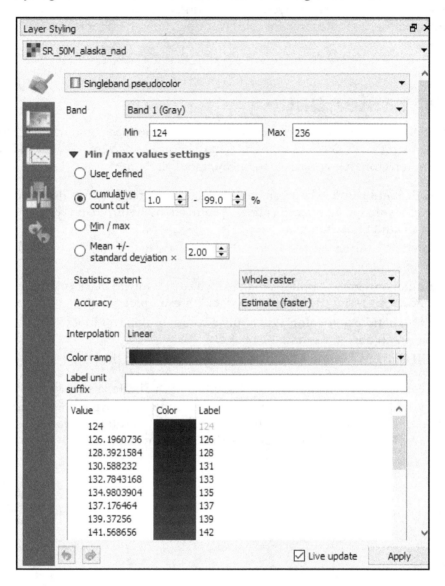

Styling a raster using a Singleband pseudocolor renderer

When working with continuous raster data, it is worth adjusting the settings so they fit your data. Experiment with different stretch settings and color ramps to best explain the data.

The `landcover` data is displayed on loading with **Paletted/Unique** values **Symbology**. As this is discrete data (it has defined classes), this is the most suitable **Symbology** type to display the `landcover` data. You can adjust the class colors by double-clicking on a color. This will open the color picker tool in the **Layer Styling** Panel, which provides several ways to adjust the color. This is shown in the following screenshot:

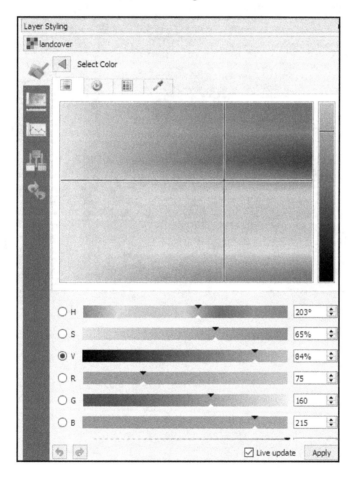

The color picker in QGIS

After selecting the most appropriate colour for a class, click on **Apply**. In this case, we don't know what each class represents, so choosing a colour is arbitrary at this point. Back in the **Layer Styling** panel, we can assign text to our labels, which is very useful when we produce maps with this data. As you make a change in the **Layer Styling** Panel, the map/layer panel will update in real time. This is shown in the following screenshot:

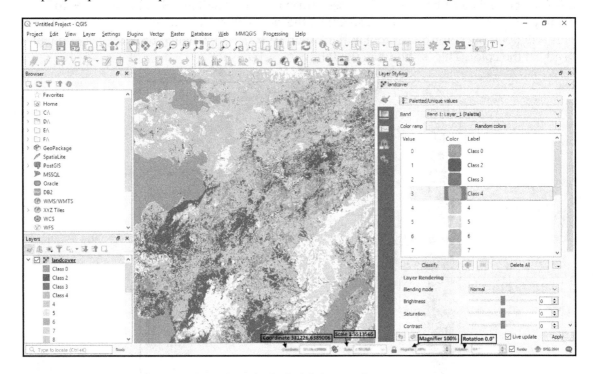

An overview of styling the landcover raster file

The Raster Toolbar

Turn on **Raster Toolbar** via **View** | **Toolbars** | **Raster Toolbar**. This is shown in the following screenshot:

Raster Toolbar

You can use this toolbar to stretch your continuous raster data (for example, DEM or satellite image data). This is done with the first four buttons shown previously, using a variety of stretches. On the last four buttons, you can increase/decrease the brightness of the raster and increase/decrease the contrast. This toolbar provides handy tools to quickly adjust your data. However, if you want more control, then use the **Layer Styling** Panel as previously demonstrated.

Saving styles

Styling data to be presented in a map can take significant time and you may wish to reuse and/or adapt your created styles in the future. This can be done by saving your style as a style file. To do this, right-click on a layer and select **Properties**.

In the lower-left corner of the **Layer Properties** dialog box is a button called **Style**, shown in the following screenshot:

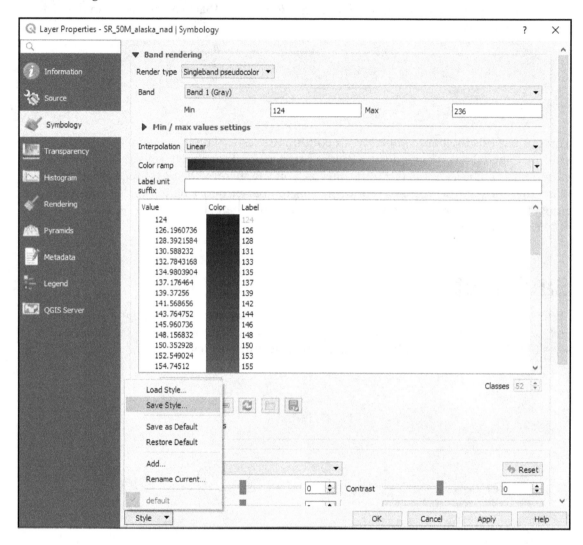

Saving a style

Select **Save Style**. There are three options for saving a style. You can save the `.qml` file to your project directory, you can save the style as an SLD (Styled Layer Descriptor file commonly used to style raster data online, in GeoServer for example), or you can save it directly into a GeoPackage. In this case, I have chosen to save it as a `.qml` file, with all the categories turned on, in my project directory. Click on **OK** to close the **Layer Properties** dialog box. Right-click on the layer and, select **Remove Layer** to remove it from the project. Now, add the layer back in and the styling will be set to default. Right-click on the layer and from the **Style** button, select **Load Style** and select the style just created.

Save your project. In the next chapter, we will use this styled data to make a map.

Summary

We have looked at styling both vector and raster data. We have used the **Layer Styling** Panel to make styling interactive. We looked at some ways to style polygons, lines, and points within QGIS. Then, we moved on to look at the ways to style both continuous and discrete raster data. Finally, we showed how to save the styles and apply them to layers.

In the next chapter, we will look at using labels to add additional information and then creating a map that can be printed or exported to a file so it can be shared.

5

Creating Maps

0In this chapter, we will be creating maps using QGIS. We will use the styling and the data from the previous chapter. We will look at labeling features, before building a map using the data. QGIS is very good at creating maps. Have a look at this gallery to get an idea of the capabilities of QGIS: `https://www.flickr.com/groups/qgis/pool/`.

The topics covered in this chapter are as follows:

- Labeling
- Creating maps
- Saving and exporting maps
- Creating an Atlas
- Building a web map

Labeling

Open the QGIS project we built in `Chapter 4`, *Styling Data*. We will be using it to build a map. Turn on the **Label Toolbar** by selecting **View** | **Toolbars** and select **Label Toolbar**. **Label Toolbar** is shown as follows:

Labeling toolbar

There are eight buttons on this toolbar; in order, these are the following:

- Clicking on Layer Labeling Options will open the **Layer Styling** Panel and the label tab by default
- Layer Diagram Options
- Highlight Pinned Labels and Diagrams

- Pin/Unpin Labels And Diagrams
- Show/Hide Labels And Diagrams
- Move Label and Diagram
- Rotate Label
- Change Label, used for label editing

Make sure that the `Airports` layer is selected in the **Layers** panel. Click on the layer labeling button on **Label Toolbar**. This will open the **Layer Styling** Panel; we used this in the previous chapter to style our layers. Choose **Single labels** and the label with **NAME** to label all `Airports`. I have reduced the **Size** of the text from **10.0000** to **8.0000** points. Make sure that the checkbox next to **Live update** is ticked so any updates can be seen as they are made. This is shown in the following screenshot:

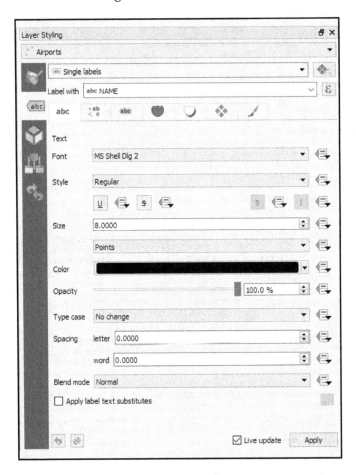

Layer Styling Panel—label design focus

These are the default labeling options. Any changes you make will be instantly seen in the map. Not all labels will be placed perfectly. A good method is to try to get as many labels in the best location possible using the **Placement** tab, and then manually move individual labels if they are still not located optimally.

With the labels tab open, select the **Placement** tab (the icon with four arrows pointing north, south, east, and west). Choose the radio button next to **Offset from point** and click the top middle quadrant in the display. This will move all the labels directly north (as you view your map) from the `Airports` icon. Adjust **Offset X,Y** to **0.0000,-2.0000** to exaggerate the distance from the icon. This is shown in the following screenshot:

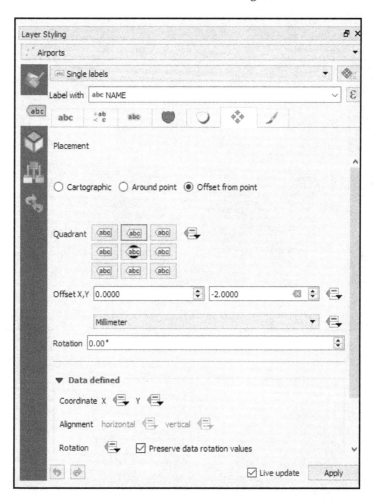

Layer Styling Panel—label Placement focus

Now that we have placed the labels, let's style them using some of the options available to us. Click on the buffer tab (the icon shows abc with a blue background). Next, check the box next to **Draw text buffer**. This helps our labels stand out more from the map. Click on the customize effects button, check the box next to **Drop Shadow**, and set its **Opacity** to **50.0%**. This is shown in the following screenshot:

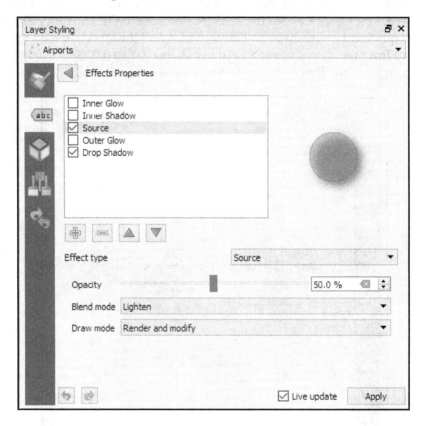

Layer Styling Panel—label Effects Properties

The map now looks like this:

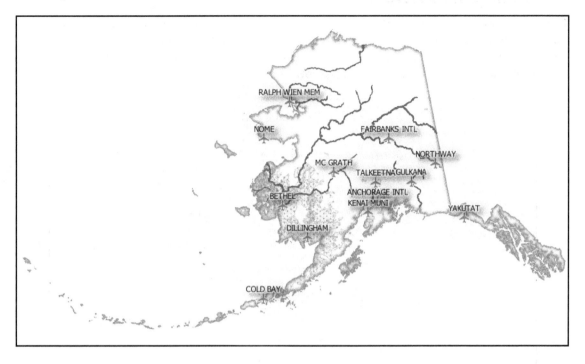

Map with layers added

As you can see, there is an issue with labels near the Anchorage International Airport. Let's use the interactive **Label Toolbar** to move these labels manually. There are still some labels not being displayed; in the next section, we will move them manually.

Manually moving labels

To interactively move a label, click on the Move Label and Diagram button on **Label Toolbar** and accept ID as the primary key. Next, click on a label and move it. As you click and drag a label, a placement box appears in green where the new location of the label will be. This is shown in the following screenshot:

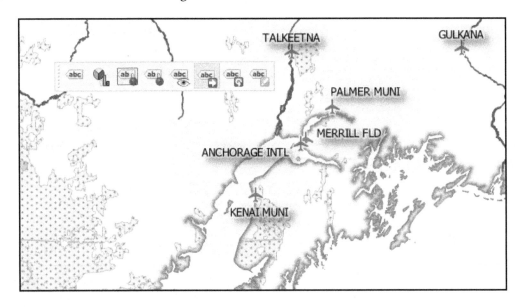

Placing labels

Keep zooming in and out of the map to ensure your labels are placed where best suited to your data. You have many other options that we will not cover in this quick start guide, but rotating (as shown highlighted on **Label Toolbar** as follows) is useful, especially on linear features:

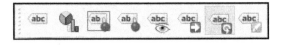

Label Toolbar

The final button on the right of **Label Toolbar** allows you to change the individual properties of one label at a time; size, color, and font size can all be set on a label-by-label basis. Your map will look similar to the following screenshot:

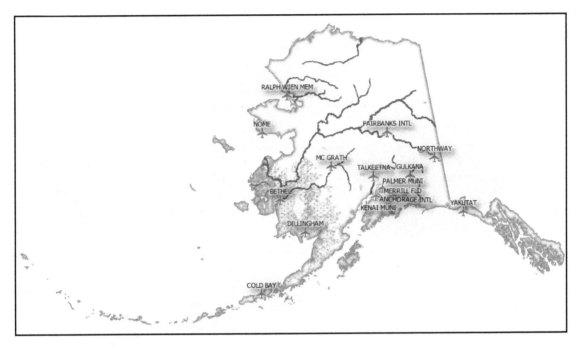

Label placement with adjustment

If you wanted to label rivers and the grassland areas, apply labels using the same tool we have just described.

We are now ready to bring this all together and make a map.

Making a map in QGIS

Click on **Project** | **New Print Layout** (or click the corresponding button on **Project Toolbar**).

In the **Create print layout Title** dialog box (shown as follows), give your new, empty map a title and click **OK**:

Creating a new print layout

You will now have an empty canvas on which we will build our map. Add your map to the layout canvas via the menu by going to **Add Item | Add Map**. Then, click and drag the mouse to draw on the canvas in the location you want to put your map. This will add an **Item** called **Map 1**; we will add more items later. This is shown in the following screenshot:

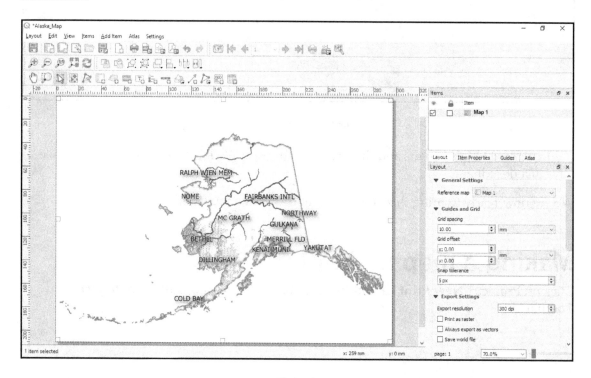

Map layout

Please note that for ease of reading this book, the label size has been increased.
For this reason you will find that the screen shots are slightly different to your screen.

With **Map 1** selected, click on the **Item Properties** tab and set the scale to 12000000, as this will display all our data on the page. Ensure that **Toolbox Toolbar** is enabled (**View** | **Toolbars** | **Toolbox**). This is a very useful toolbar as it allow us to design our page. Click on the Move Item Content button, highlighted as follows:

Move item button—used to move an item on the map

This tool allows us to move the data in the map around so it best fits the page. When you are happy it is in the right place, click on Pan Map (the hand icon).

To add a legend, click on the add legend button. Draw an area where the legend will appear on the map. The legend may appear messy at first, but we can adjust it in **Item Properties**. Make sure that the legend is selected in the **Items** panel, and then from the **Item Properties** tab add a title (**Legend**) and uncheck the auto update checkbox. We can remove any layers appearing in the legend that we don't want. In the map, the Hillshade and landcover rasters are still there. To remove these, click on the layer name and then click on the red minus button to remove it from the legend. If you wanted to add a layer back, then click on the green cross to bring up a list of layers to select. To finish the legend, scroll down **Item Properties** and expand **Fonts**.

Here, set **Title font** to bold. The map now looks like this:

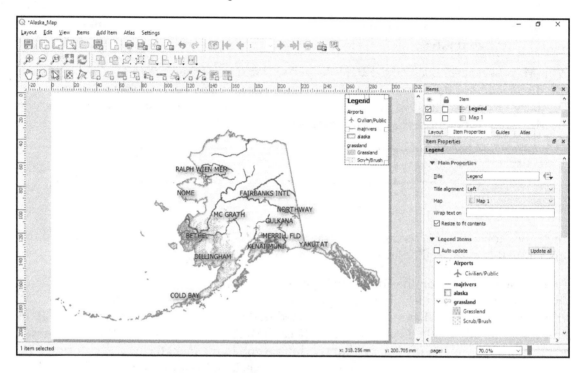

Map layout with Legend added

Next, add a scalebar. In **Toolbox Toolbar**, select the scalebar tool and click and drag a new scalebar to the lower-right corner of the map. In **Item Properties** for the scalebar, set **Style** as **Double Box** and the units to **Miles**. Change the **Label for units** value from **mi** to **Miles**.

Add a north arrow by clicking **Add Item | Add Picture** and draw a box to contain your north arrow. Use the item properties of the north arrow to point to the location on your computer where the QGIS SVG files are stored. In this example, I am using `C:\OSGeo4W64\apps\qgis\svg\arrows/NorthArrow_11.svg`.

Now, we need to add a title and a description. To add text to this map, select **Add Item | Add label**. Draw a box in the lower-left corner, and in the **Item Properties** window, copy the following text:

```
<h1>A QGIS built map of Alaska</h1>
<h2>This map was created in QGIS 3.4</h2>
<p>We used the following data</p>
<ul><li>Airports</li>
<li>Grassland</li>
```

```
<li>Rivers</li>
<li>Alaska boundary</li></ul>
```

Click on **Render as HTML**.

To finish, we can set a background color for the map. Select **Map 1** in the **Items** panel and scroll to the background options in the **Item Properties**. Choose a neutral color; I have selected a light gray. Adjust the transparency to a suitable level so it doesn't distract the viewer. Select the legend in the **Items** panel and set the background to the same color as the map background.

Finally, from the **Toolbox Toolbar**, click on the Add Shape icon. Choose a rectangle and draw around the title. Select it as the item and, in **Item Properties**, change the fill to no fill and the boarder to black (it will be black by default). Then, set **Corner radius** to **3.00**, so the corners are rounded in the textbox.

Your map will look similar to the following screenshot:

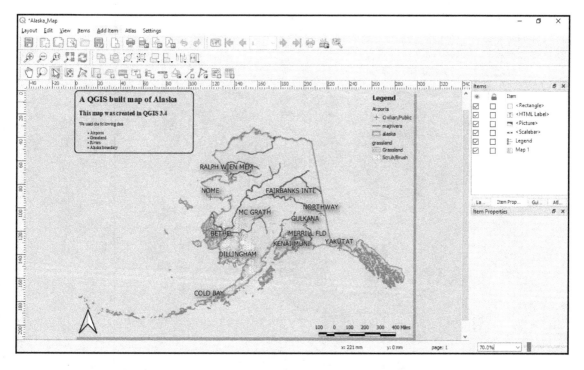

Map layout updated in QGIS 3.4

Save your map via **Layout** | **Save Project**. To save it as `.pdf`, click **Layout** | **Export as pdf**. You may need to adjust the export settings, such as dpi values, to make the optimal map output. To do this, click on the **Layout** tab on the right of the screen (next to **Item Properties**). On this screen, you will have the option to change a variety of settings. The **Layout** tab is shown in the following screenshot:

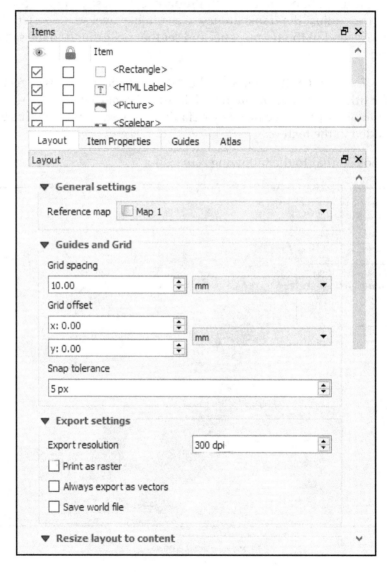

Layout settings

Creating an Atlas

Close the layout we have just created and return to the QGIS main project screen. In this example, we are going to create an Atlas of maps of the locations around civilian airports. To do this, use the **NAME** field, which contains only civilian airports. Let's create a new basic layout to show this functionality. We can do this by selecting **Project | New Print Layout**, or via **Layout Manager Project | Layout Manager**. Let's choose **Layout Manager**. This is a useful dialog box that lists all of our created layouts within a QGIS project. It is shown in the following screenshot:

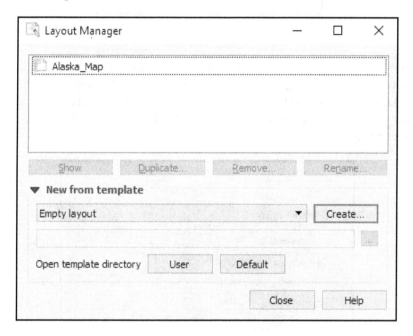

QGIS Layout Manager

Select **Empty layout** and click on **Create** to open a new blank template. I am going to call my new layout `Airport_Atlas`:

Create a new print layout

As we did when creating the Alaska map, select the add new map to layout button, and click and drag to fill the map page with the data from the QGIS project. From the menu bar, select **Atlas | Atlas settings** and then check the box next to **Generate an atlas**. Now, select **Coverage layer** as `Airports` and **Page name** as **NAME**. This will tell the Atlas to create one page per airport name:

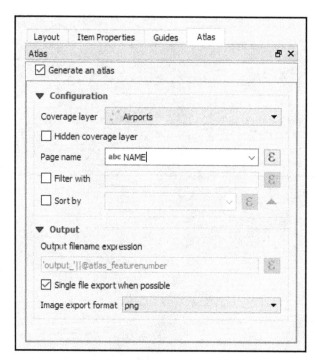

Options for generating an Atlas

In the **Item Properties** tab, make sure that **Controlled by atlas** is checked; this will mean the scale/view will adjust to each feature. Next, ensure that the **Atlas** toolbar is turned on. The toolbar is shown in the following screenshot:

Atlas toolbar

Click on the preview button in the **Atlas** toolbar and use the arrows to scroll through the proposed Atlas. This is shown in the following screenshot:

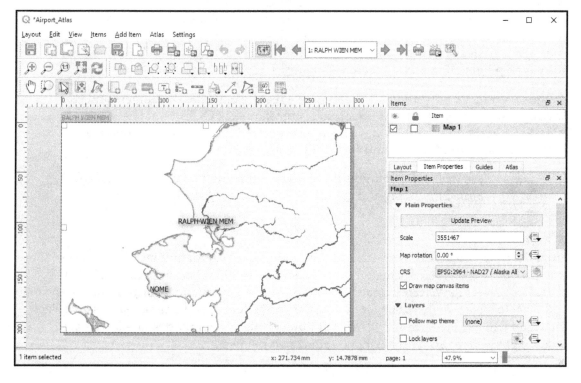

Map created in the Atlas function

The scale may need adjusting to suit your needs. You can add a title, legend, scale bar, and north arrow as we did in the previous example. Once you have finished, select **Atlas |
Export Atlas** from the menu as `.pdf` and save to disk. This is a simple example, but
it shows the basics of creating an Atlas; you only need to build one layout to do it. Save and
close your layout when finished.

Finally, in this chapter, we will have a quick look at creating a map for the web.

Creating a web map

We can do more than just create printed or static digital maps. By creating a web map, a
user has the ability to have more interaction with a map online. QGIS has a plugin that will
allow you to display your data as a web map. This provides another option for sharing
your maps. In this brief example, we will introduce QGIS plugins and how the
`qgis2web` plugin allows us to create web maps.

Plugins are a really powerful and collaborative feature of QGIS. Developers and companies
have created many plugins that extend the core features of QGIS. Some have been so
integral to workflows that they have been incorporated into the main software. From the
Plugins menu, select **Manage and Install Plugins**.

We will look at plugins more in the following two chapters, Chapter 6,
Spatial Processing and Chapter 7, *Expanding QGIS 3*.

From the plugin manager, with the **ALL** tab selected, search for and install `qgis2web`. Once
installed, close the plugin manager. In the menu, there should be an option called **Web**.
From here, select **qgis2web | create web map**. Adjust **Layers and Groups** to match the map
you wish to create. In this example, `Airports`, `majrivers`, and `alaska` layers are selected.
This map will use the `Leaflet` JavaScript library; this is a library designed to create
lightweight web maps. A screenshot of **qgis2web** follows:

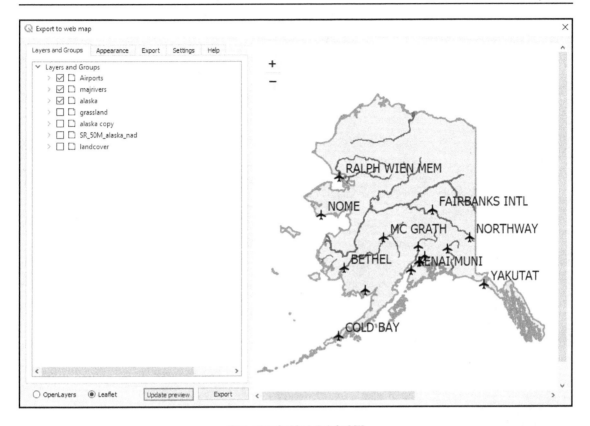

The overview of qgis2web plugin for QGIS

When you are happy with the configuration, click on the **Export** button; this will save the web map at the location specified as the Export folder. Then, open the resulting web map in your web browser. You can copy the contents in the Export folder to a web server to publish the map. The qgis2web plugin is a very efficient way of creating web maps.

Summary

In this chapter, we have built maps with QGIS. We first looked at labeling options, both with rules and then interactively changing individual labels. Then, we built a map using the data we styled in the previous chapter. We then looked at how to create an Atlas, before finally looking at options to export the map to the web using the qgis2web plugin.

In the next chapter, we will look at spatial analysis, helping to derive more detailed spatial information about data.

6
Spatial Processing

In this chapter, we'll be performing spatial analysis using QGIS. We'll use the data from the GeoPackage that we used in the previous data chapters. Firstly, we'll look at the Processing Toolbox and then move on to some individual tools and spatially query our data.

The following topics will be covered in this chapter:

- The Processing Toolbox
- Spatial queries
- Analyzing data
- Raster-based analysis

The Processing Toolbox

From the **Processing** menu, select **Toolbox**. The **Processing Toolbox** is shown as follows:

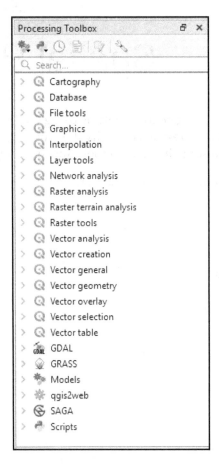

Processing Toolbox

At the top of the **Processing Toolbox,** there is a toolbar. In this toolbar, the first button is used to call the model builder and the second button opens the Python scripting tools, both of which we'll come to later. The next four buttons, in order, show **History**, **Results Viewer**, **Edit Features In-Place** (this button shows tools that *filters to display only algorithms that allow in-place modification of the geometries*), and processing settings. Under this toolbar is the search feature; using this feature, you can quickly find processing tools and run them.

In this chapter, we'll use these tools to analyze and work with our data. We'll use some of the tools in the Processing Toolbox to answer some spatial or GIS-type questions.

Create a new empty QGIS project. Load in the following layers from the GeoPackage:

- regions
- pipelines

What regions intersect pipelines?

We can answer this with a spatial query. In QGIS, this tool is called **Select by Location**; search for this term in the **Processing Toolbox**, then double-click on the tool to open the dialog box. We want to use this tool to select all of the features from the regions layer that **intersect** with pipelines. The input will look like this:

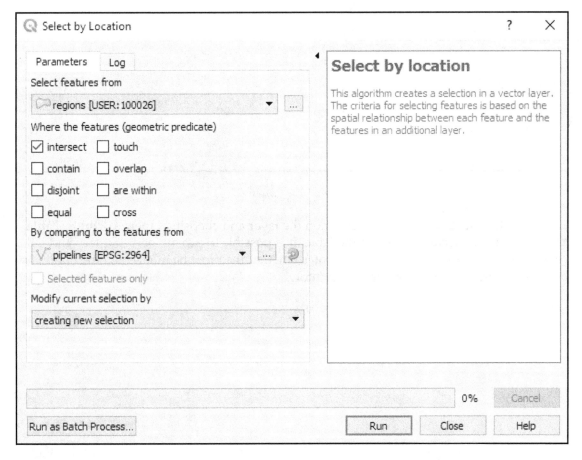

Select by Location tool

The output in QGIS will look like this:

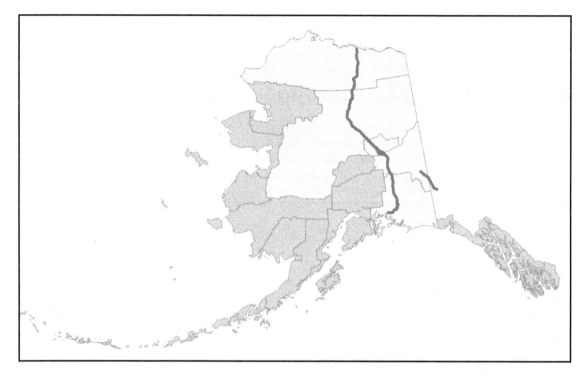

Selected regions highlighted

Open the attribute table by right-clicking on the layer and choosing **Open Attribute Table**. You will see the selected regions in the table. It is possible to expand on this query and create a field in the `regions` layer that notes whether the pipeline intersected the region or not. To do this, we can use the field calculator.

Let's add a field called `Pipeline` and assign the value one if the pipeline runs through the region and zero if it doesn't. In the attribute table, click on the open field calculator button (the icon is an abacus). Fill in the **Field Calculator** as follows. Make sure the checkbox next to **Only update 5 selected features** is selected:

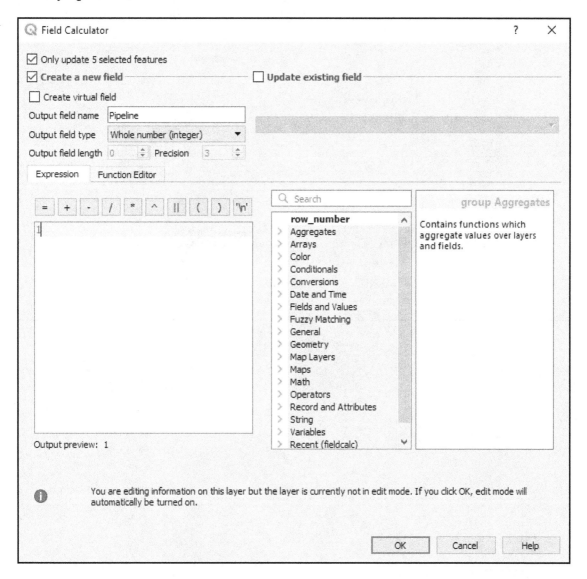

The field calculator

Click on **OK** and then open the attribute table; you will see a new field called `Pipeline`. This is shown as follows:

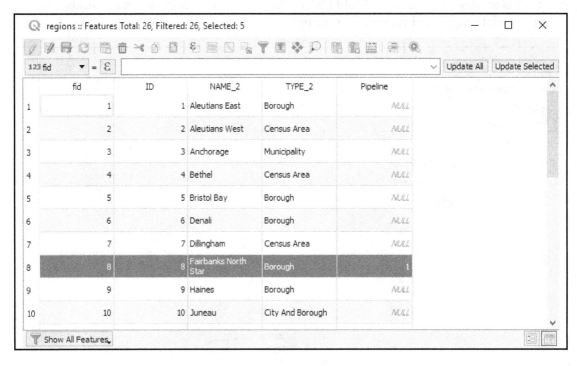

Attribute table with selected feature(s)

We need to add the value zero now to all of the other fields. Invert the selection (the button looks like a yellow triangle underneath a grey triangle). Choose the `Pipeline` field from the drop-down menu and set the value equal to 0. Click on **Update Selected**. The value to change is shown in the following screenshot:

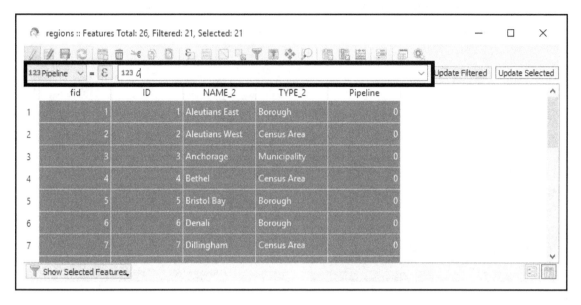

Update existing field in the field calculator

Click on **OK**. Now, the `Pipeline` field has either zero (not impacted) or one (impacted). Clear the selection and untoggle the editing. We could use the styling skills from `Chapter 4`, *Styling Data*, to symbolize the region layer based on the newly created `Pipeline` field.

What buildings and settlements are within 15,000 feet of the pipeline?

To answer this question, we need to perform a buffer on the pipeline and then select the points in the **popp** layer that fall inside this buffer. This is a common GIS query, and the method shown here should be applicable to any similar query you might have about your data. Load the **popp** layer into the map.

Search in the **Processing Toolbox** for **Buffer**. Double-click to open the tool. Select the `pipelines` layer and set the buffer **Distance** to `15000` feet. Check the box next to **Dissolve result**; this will merge any adjacent or overlapping features into one feature. For the output, choose the GeoPackage that we supplied with this book containing this `alaska` layers. The **Buffer** dialog should look as follows:

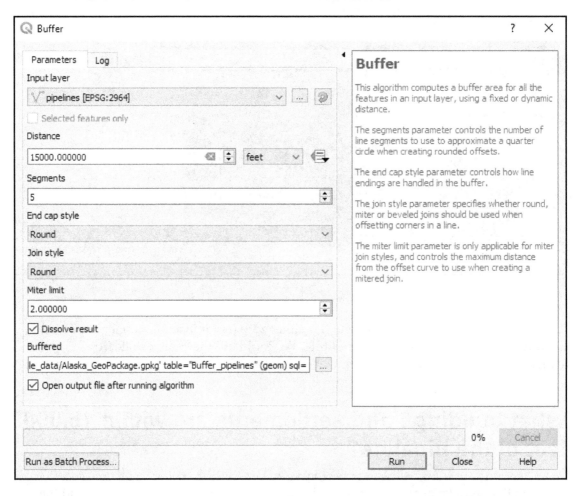

The Buffer tool

Click on **Run**. Click on **Close** when the tool has finished. On the map, we should now have a buffer of the pipelines. Use the **Select by Location** tool as before, but this time select the points in the **popp** layer that are within this newly created buffer. The dialog should look similar to the following screenshot:

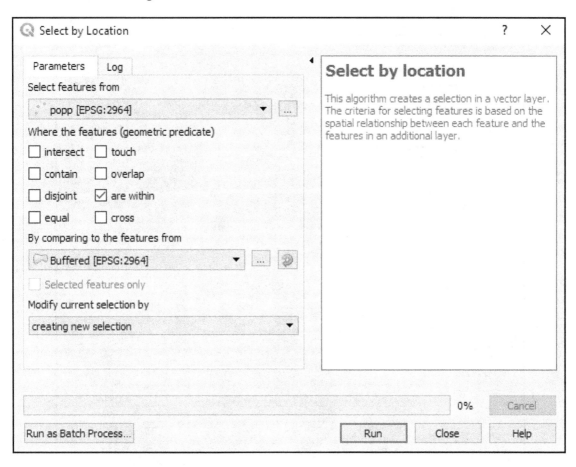

Select by Location tool

After clicking **Run**, close the tool and inspect the map. This query results in 49 features being selected. To write these out to a new layer, right-click on the **popp** layer in the layer panel and select **Export | Save Selected Features As**. Save the selected features to a new layer in the GeoPackage called Popp_in_pipeline_corridor. This is shown in the following screenshot:

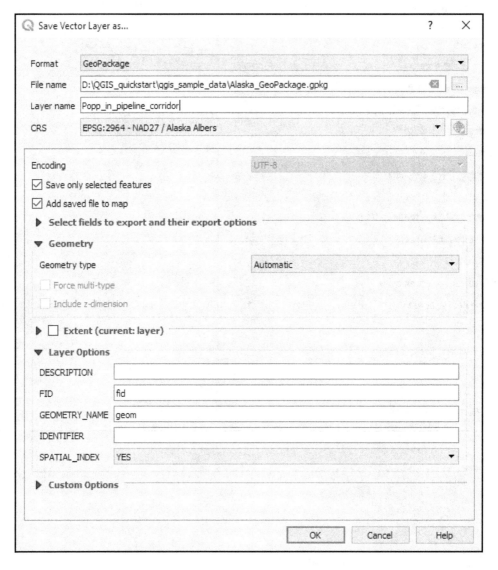

Saving the layer

Click on **OK** and, in the layer panel, turn off all of the layers apart from this one and the regions. Your map should look like the following:

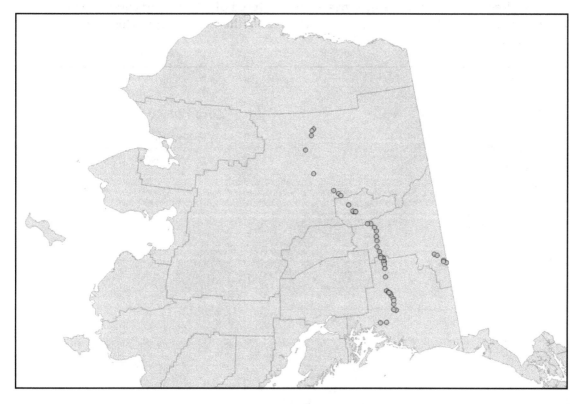

All of the popp points 15,000 feet from the pipeline

Similar to the first question, this query is common in GIS. Instead of settlements and buildings in a pipeline corridor, you might be dealing with address points for customers within *x* distance of a new shop that you might wish to contact to let them know about a new offer.

What is the distribution landcover types inside the buffered pipeline?

This question is one where we combine both raster and vector data to provide an answer. We might want to know whether the pipeline is going through a protected area and how much of that area is impacted.

Load the `landcover.img` dataset into the **Layers** panel. To answer this question, we'll use a tool call **Zonal Histogram**. Search for it in the toolbox. Set **Raster layer** as the `landcover` layer, set **Vector layer containing zones** as the **Buffered** pipelines, and choose to prefix the zones with the word `Terrain_`. Save your changes to the GeoPackage. This is shown in the following screenshot:

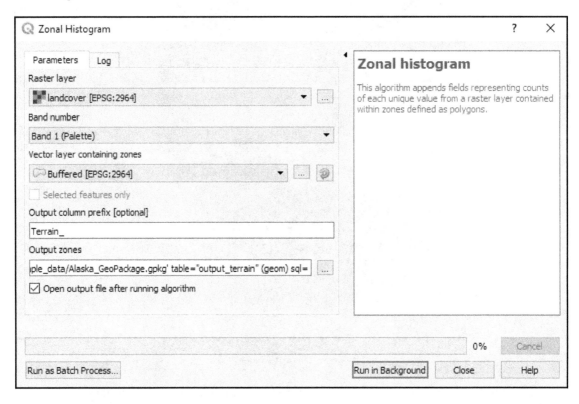

Zonal histogram tool

Click on **Run in Background** and close when finished. A new layer with one feature will have been added to the **Layers** panel. Right-click on this layer and open the attribute table. The table only has one feature because we dissolved the buffer when we created it. The resulting table looks like the following screenshot:

The attribute table generated by the zonal stats tool

We can see the field with `Terrain_x`, where x corresponds to the value in the `landcover` raster. The most impacted terrain of the pipeline was `Terrain_9`.

In `Chapter 7`, *Expanding QGIS 3*, we'll look at how we can combine the tools in questions 2 and 3 into a model to automate these processes. This would allow us to just run one tool.

Let's now move on to terrain modeling with raster data.

Raster analysis

Create a new QGIS project and load into the map the `landcover.img` file. We'll use this layer to demonstrate a couple of the many raster processing tools in QGIS. On load, we have landcover classes with values ranging from 0 to 13. The value zero appears to correspond to water. In this example, we're going to set all of the values that are equal to zero to nodata. In GIS we would set raster data to no data when we have data that we don't want to use or display.

To change the 0 values in the `Landcover` dataset to nodata, select **Raster | Conversion | Translate (Convert Format)** as shown in the following screenshot:

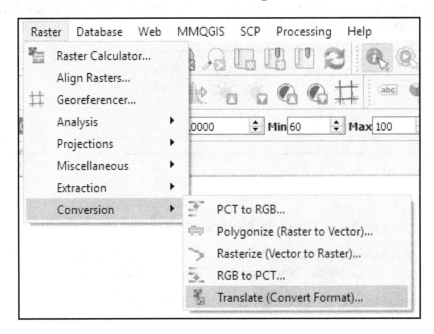

Calling the Translate tool

The **Translate** tool is very helpful to convert rasters into different data types and formats. It's built on the GDAL translate tool; you can read about the options with `gdal_translate` here: `https://www.gdal.org/gdal_translate.html`. With the **Translate** tool open in QGIS, select the `landcover` layer as **Input layer** and set **Assign a specific nodata value to the output bands** to 0. Save the output box labeled **Converted** as `Landcover_Null.tif`. This is shown in the following screenshot:

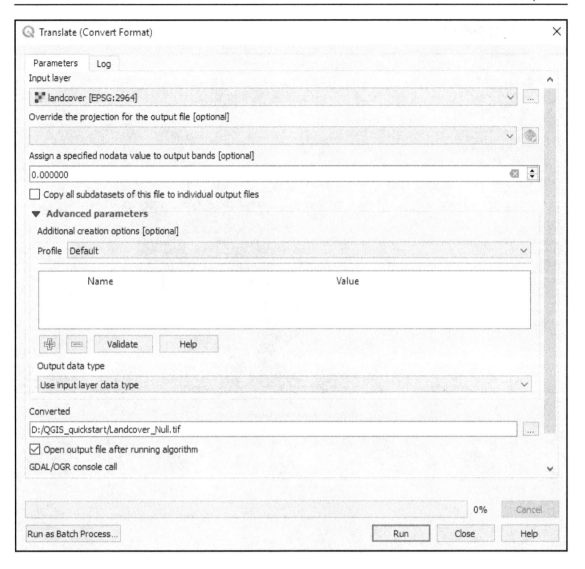

Using the Translate tool to set a no data value

The resulting raster will look like this:

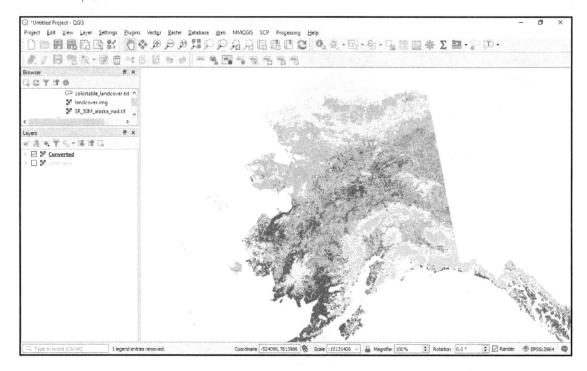

Landcover with the values 0 set to no data

Using this newly created layer, we'll reclassify this raster dataset based on a conditional statement in **Raster Calculator**. We'll set every terrain will a value greater than or equal to five to zero and everything else to one. Open **Raster Calculator** and enter the following in the **Raster Calculator Expression** window: `"Converted@1" >= 5`, and save as `Landcover_Null_reclassified.tif` as shown in the following screenshot:

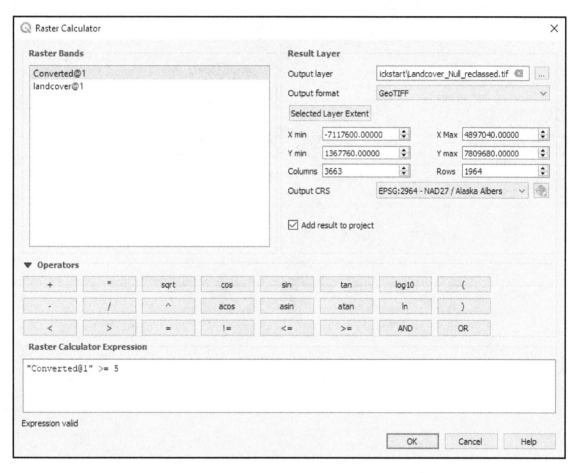

Conditional statements in the Raster Calculator

The resulting binary raster will look like the following screenshot:

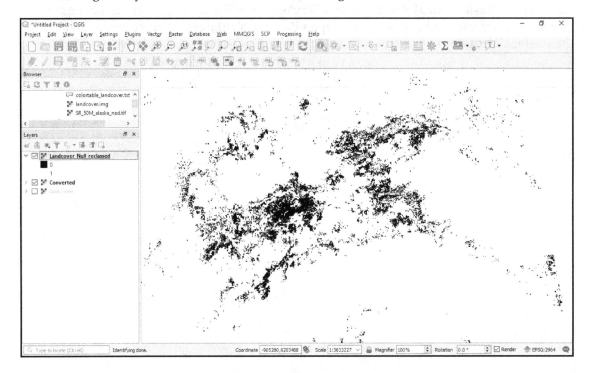

Conditional raster generated from the Raster Calculator

You might not have expected this result as the values 0 are in black and 1 are displayed in white. We could alter this; to do so, we need to change the rendering for the values of 1 to be shaded and everything else to be transparent (or white). Right-click on the `Landcover_Null_reclassed` layer and select **Properties**. Set **Render type** to **Paletted/Unique values,** click on **Classify** and adjust the values of 1 to red and 0 to transparent, as shown in the following screenshot:

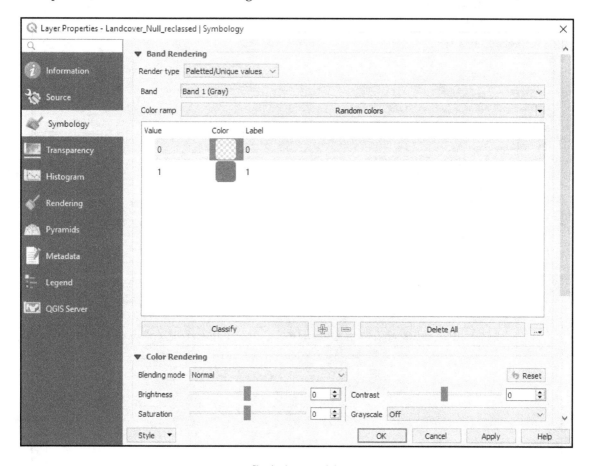

Changing the raster rendering

In the next section, we'll look at converting this raster into a vector dataset.

Converting into vectors

Reclassifying rasters is useful for many visualization and processing workflows but also useful for converting data into vectors. From the **Raster** menu, select **Conversion | Polygonize (Raster to Vector)**, which will open the **Raster to Vector** tool. Save the **Vectorized** layer as a new GeoPackage layer called `vectorised_terrains.gpkg` as shown in the following screenshot:

Polygonize tool

This will take a little while to run as the raster is quite complex. Once finished, you'll have a vector layer that will look similar to the following screenshot:

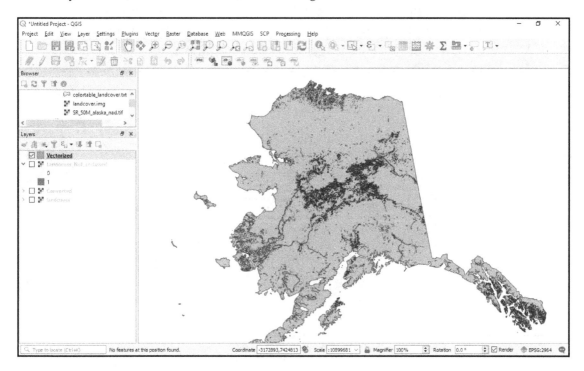

The resulting vector layer created from the conditional raster

The newly created vector dataset will have features with a DN field equal to either 1 or 0. In this case, we aren't interested in any of the DN values equal to 0. Open the attribute table of the layer and select the values in the DN field that are equal to 0 using the select features. Using an expression (click on the tenth button from the left in the attribute table). Click on **Select features** and then **Close**, as shown in the following screenshot:

Editing the vectorized layer

Click on the Toggle editing mode button in the attribute table (first button on the left) and then click on the red trashcan to delete the selected values. Click on the Toggle editing mode to turn off editing and save the edits. The final data should now look similar to the following:

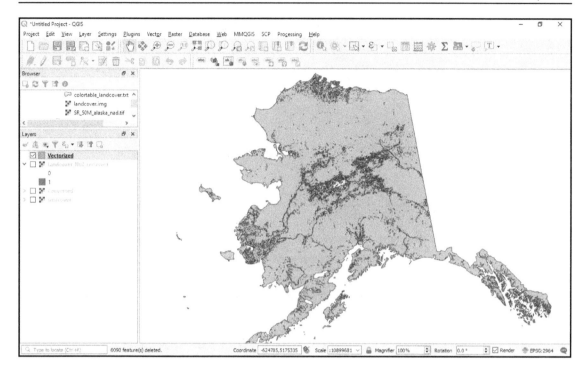

Final vectorized terrain layer

There are many raster analysis tools in the QGIS processing toolbox that we could use. For example, if you have access to a DEM, you could create slope maps and other types of terrain analysis; search for **Raster Terrain Analysis** in the **Processing Toolbox**.

Summary

In this chapter, we've dipped our toes into the Processing Toolbox in QGIS. We asked questions about our data. We used simple GIS processes and tools in QGIS to derive answers from our data. The power of GIS lies in its data. We also looked at both vector- and raster-based queries.

In the next chapter, we'll look at extending this by using the model builder to chain common processing tools together, before looking at Plugins and the Python Console.

Expanding QGIS 3

7

In this final chapter, we will look at expanding QGIS. We will look at combining tools into a model using the model builder. This effectively allows us to build our own reusable model, using parameters we either hardcode in or leave to the user to adjust. We will look at the ever-increasing range of plugins, before finally taking a brief look at the Python command line, where we can create scripts in the future as confidence grows with QGIS.

These are the topics covered in this chapter:

- Model builder
- Plugins
- Python command line

Model builder

You may recall that in the Chapter 6, *Spatial Processing* we ran several tools to utilize the zonal histogram answer to the distribution of terrains (Landcover) in a buffered pipeline corridor. Open a new QGIS project and load in the Pipeline layer and the Landcover.

To create a model, go to **Processing | Graphical Modeler** to open the modeler, where we can select from different **Inputs** and **Algorithms** for our model. **Graphical Modeler** is shown in the following screenshot:

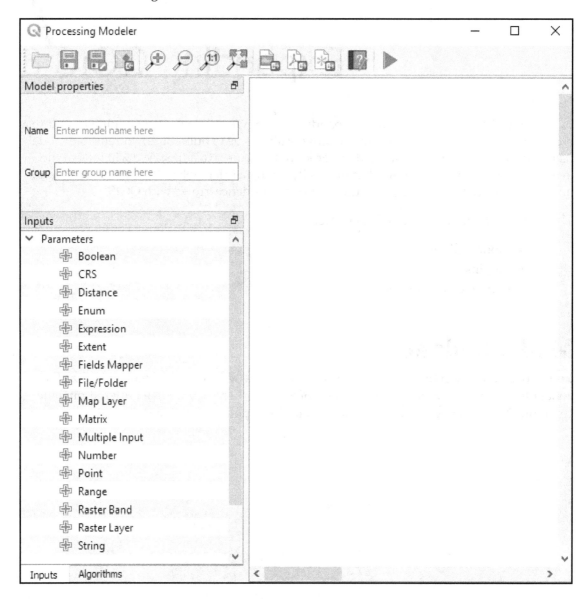

The Graphical Modeler

Select the **Inputs** tab and choose **Vector Layer**. Add a new parameter called `Pipeline` and set **Geometry type** to **Line**; this is shown in the following screenshot:

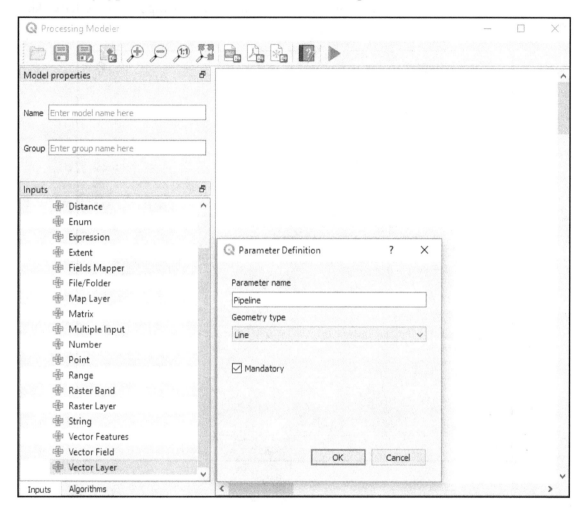

Creating a Pipeline attribute as a Geometry type—Line

Click on **OK**. Now, add **Raster Layer** and call it `Landcover`. In the **Algorithms** tab, we can use the filter at the top to narrow down our search for the correct algorithm. Search for `buffer` and double-click to open the algorithm. Fill in **Distance** as `15000` and check the box to make sure the layer is dissolved.

Now, search for and open the **Zonal histogram** tool and change the prefix to `Terrain_`. This is our final output so tell the model it is the final result. The final output is what is returned to the user once the model has been successfully run. The inputs should look like the following dialog box:

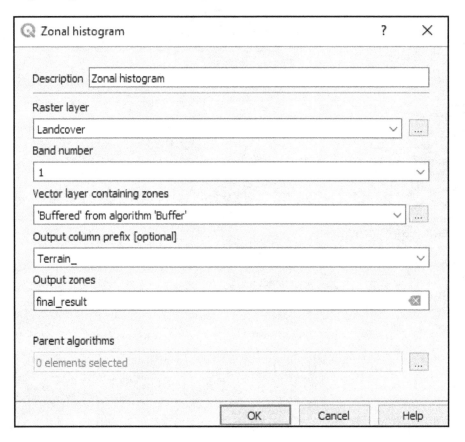

Zonal histogram tool

Click on **OK**. To finish the model, we need to enter a model **Name**
(Pipeline_impact_terrain) and a **Group** name (QuickStart_QGIS). Processing will
use the **Group** name to organize all the models that we create into different toolbox groups.
The model is now complete. The finished model will look like this:

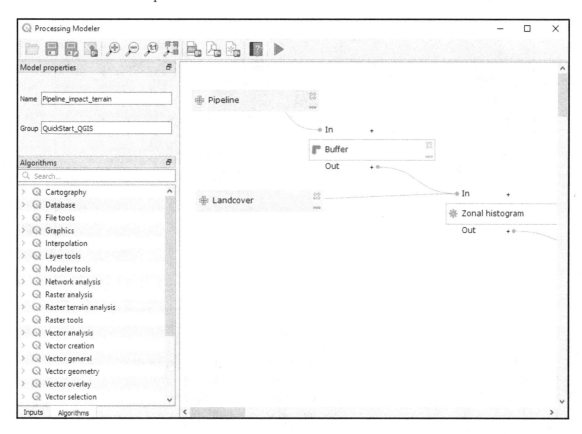

The Graphical Modeler with the model displayed

Click the save icon and save as `terrain_stats.model3`. Click on the green triangle or press *F5* to run the model. A dialog box should appear as follows:

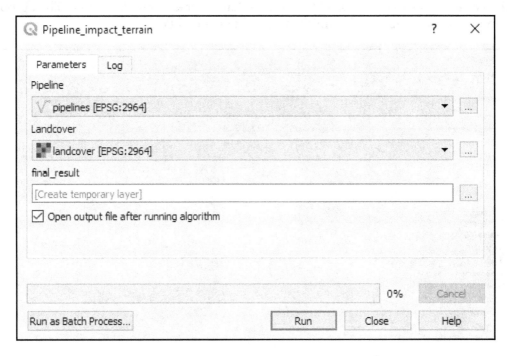

The model represented as a tool

Click on **Run** to execute the model. The pipeline output will appear in the QGIS map window. After closing the modeler, we can run the saved models from the toolbox like any other tool. Look in **Processing Toolbox** under **Models**. This newly created model will appear there, as shown in the following screenshot. It is even possible to use one model as a building block for another model:

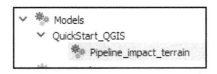

Model appears in the Processing Toolbox under Models

Another useful feature is that we can specify a layer style that needs to be automatically applied to the processing results. This default style can be set by right-clicking and selecting **Edit**, rendering styles for outputs in the context menu of the created model in the toolbox. This means that you can automate building maps if you wish.

You can share your models by giving the `.model3` file to others. This is the first step in expanding the use of QGIS. Save your project.

Plugins in QGIS

We briefly touched on plugins in `Chapter 5`, *Creating Maps*. We used qgis2web to convert our Alaska map into a web map. The top plugins by download are listed here: `https://plugins.qgis.org/plugins/popular/`. You can use this page to search for plugins or look at tags to view the different plugins and their capabilities.

Plugins are accessed via the **Plugins** menu. Some plugins are experimental. By experimental, we mean they could be unstable or in the early stages of development, but it is worth turning these on in case a plugin is available that might help your workflows; just use them with caution. From the **Plugins** dialog, choose **Settings** and check the box next to **Show also experimental plugins**:

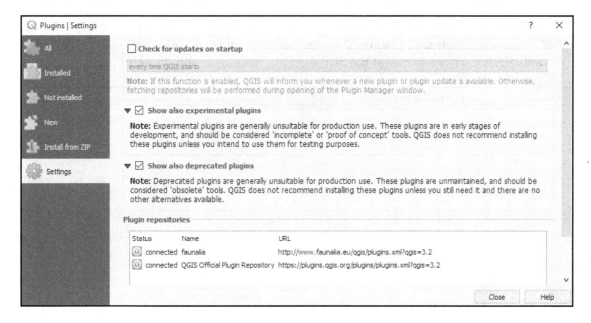

Plugin settings

Semi-Automatic Classification Plugin

The **Semi-Automatic Classification Plugin** (**SCP**) for QGIS allows for the supervised classification of remote sensing images, providing tools for the downloading, preprocessing, and postprocessing of satellite images (`https://plugins.qgis.org/plugins/SemiAutomaticClassificationPlugin/`). It is an amazingly powerful tool that significantly extends Remote Sensing functionality into QGIS.

In this example, we will use the SCP to download a `Sentinel-2` image that covers the part of Alaska that we digitized: Fire Island. At this point, please make sure you have an account with the **Copernicus Open Data Hub**. You can do this at: `https://scihub.copernicus.eu/dhus/#/self-registration`.

Open a new QGIS project and add the `OpenStreeMap` data from `XYZ Tiles` in the **Browser** panel, and then add the `Island_Outline` layer from the `Fire_Island` GeoPackage that we created in `Chapter 3`, *Creating Data*. Make sure that the map project in the status bar is set to EPSG 3857.

To install the SCP, select **Plugins** | **Manage and Install Plugins**. Click on the **All** tab, search for SCP, and click on **Install plugin**. Two new toolbars and one new panel will appear. In this example, we will look only at the SCP working toolbar, as shown as follows:

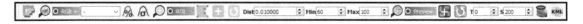

SCP Working Toolbar

Click on the button on the far left of this toolbar; this will open a dialog box, shown in the following screenshot:

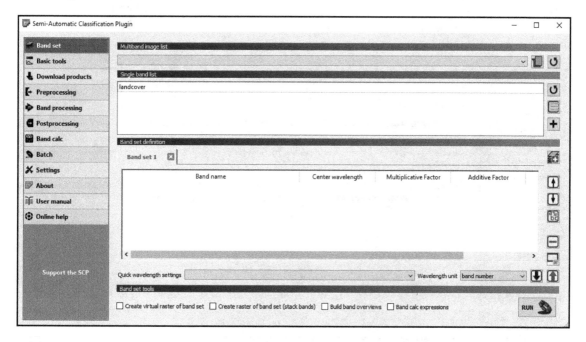

Semi-Automatic Classification Plugin dialog box

Assuming that you have an account set up with the Copernicus Open Data Hub, then click on the **Download products** menu and select the **Login data** tab. Here, enter your username and password. Next, select the **Search** tab and select Sentinel-2 from **Products list**, set the date range to November 01, 2018, to December 01, 2018, and the cloud cover to 25%, as shown in the following screenshot:

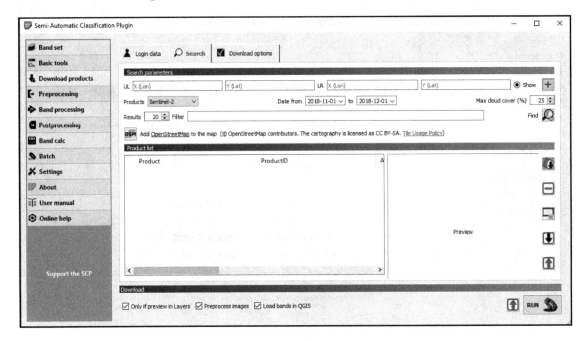

Setting the Search parameters

To define the area we are searching, click on the button with plus sign with an orange background, minimize the window, and return to the main QGIS screen. Left-click to get the **Upper Left** (**UL**) and right-click to get the **Lower Right** (**LR**). You should get a box drawn on your map as follows:

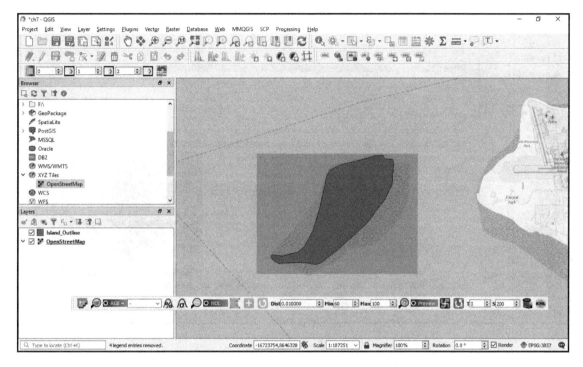

An overview of defining the search area

Go to the plugin (you can click the plugin button as before, or just maximize the SCP plugin window). If you are happy with **Search parameters**, click on the button next to **Find**. The results will be returned in **Product list**. You can click each one to find the best image. This is shown in the following screenshot:

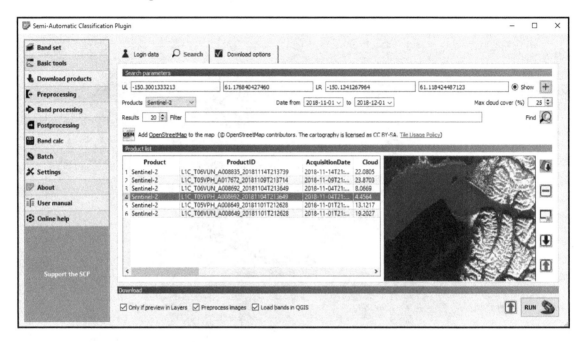

Selecting an image

If you uncheck the **Only if preview in Layers** option, at this point you could click on **Run** (bottom-right-hand corner). That will go ahead and download a large amount of data and preprocess it (correct for atmospheric effects). In this example, to save on download size, select **Download options** and choose only band 2, 3, and 4 and the ancillary data. This will allow us to create a true color satellite image. I have also turned off the **Preprocess images** options to simplify this walk-through. These options are shown in the following screenshot:

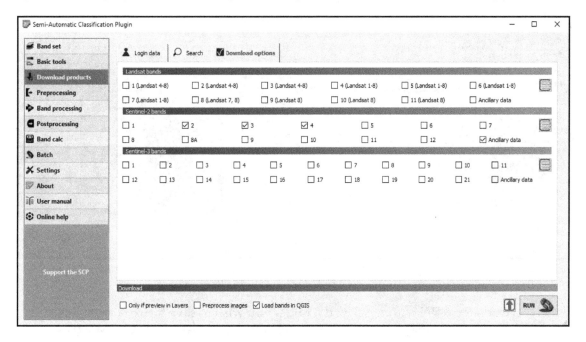

Specify the download options

Back in the **Search** tab, I have turned on the **Only if preview in Layers** option and clicked on the Display preview of highlighted images in map button. This has added my selected product to my map. This is shown in the following screenshot:

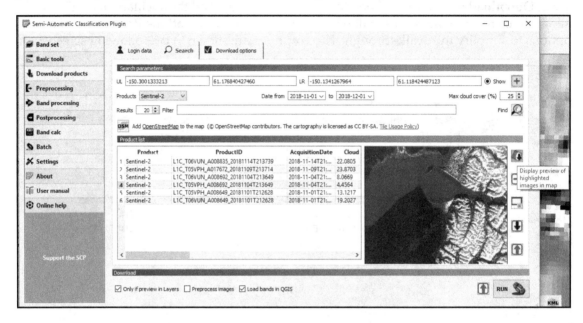

Displaying a preview in the layers via the dialog box

Finally, click on the **RUN** button, select the folder you wish to save the data in, and let the data download. When finished, you should have your Sentinel-2 images loaded as layers in QGIS. There is significantly more functionality in this plugin than covered here. If you are interested in exploring the available functionality further, including classification of satellite data with QGIS, then please visit https://fromgistors.blogspot.com/p/semi-automatic-classification-plugin.html for extensive documentation, videos, and guides.

The satellite data should be loaded into QGIS. Using **Raster Toolbar**, stretch one of the bands until you can see it (sometimes images are loaded dark, especially if there is a large amount of sea in them). Your screen should look as follows:

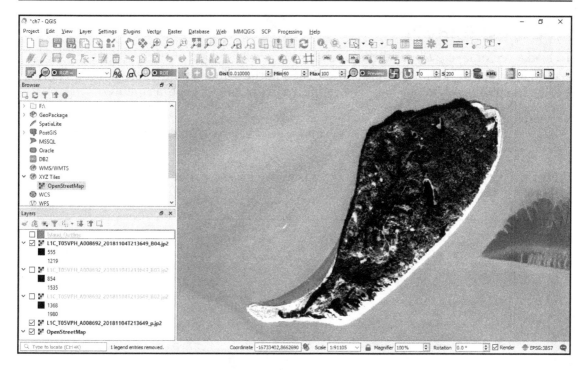

Downloaded satellite image appears in QGIS

There are many more plugins available; use **Plugin Manager** to search for and explore new tools to work with.

Using the Python command line

From the **Plugins** toolbar, select the **Python Console** button, or press *Ctrl + Alt + P*, or select **Python Console** from the **Plugins** menu.

Python has become the programming language of choice for GIS. In this book, we will just look at the basics of the QGIS API. As you become more advanced, you can use Python to develop your own plugins and custom scripts. Eventually, you could use the QGIS Python library (PyQGIS), external to QGIS, to build applications.

Open a new empty QGIS project.

Loading a layer

To load a vector layer, we use the `addVectorLayer()` function of `iface`. The `iface` class is used to access the graphical part of the QGIS interface. In the following example, I am adding `airport.shp` to the map. This is shown in one line of code, as follows:

```
Airport_layer =
iface.addVectorLayer('D:/QGIS_quickstart/qgis_sample_data/shapefiles/airpor
ts.shp','airports','ogr')
```

Press the *Enter* key and the `airports` layer is now loaded (change the path to your Shapefile):

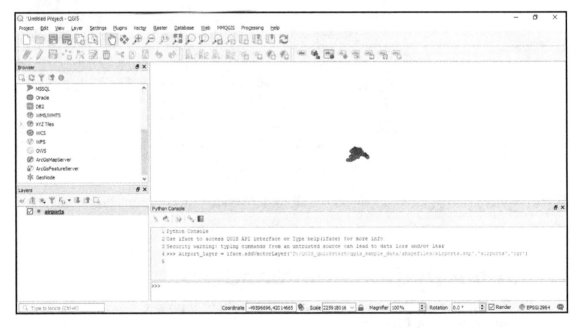

The airports Shapefile loaded into the QGIS map

Add another layer:

```
Alaska_layer =
iface.addVectorLayer('D:/QGIS_quickstart/qgis_sample_data/shapefiles/alaska
.shp','alaska','ogr')
```

We now have the `alaska` boundary and the `airports` layer added to the map.

Inspecting the layer

We can look at each layer by accessing some of the properties. To get the name of the layer, use the `.name()` function:

`Airport_layer.name()`

The output is as follows:

`'airports'`

To count the number of records in the layer, use the `featureCount()` function:

`Airport_layer.featureCount()`

The output is as follows:

`76`

To print the attributes for all these 76 layers, use a `for` loop:

```
airportFeatures = Airport_layer.getFeatures()
for feature in airportFeatures:
    print (feature.attributes())
```

Remember to use the indentation. The result will look similar to this:

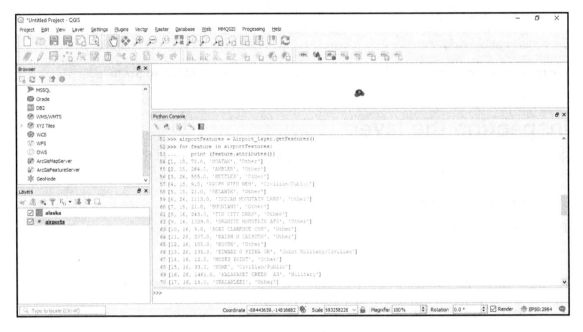

The QGIS Python Console printing out the attribute table

Scripts

The command line can get confusing. It is better to build scripts and test on the command line. Let's convert these command-line calls into a Python script. Close this project and open a new QGIS project. Open the Python Console.

Click on the Show Editor button to open a scripting window. This is shown in the following screenshot:

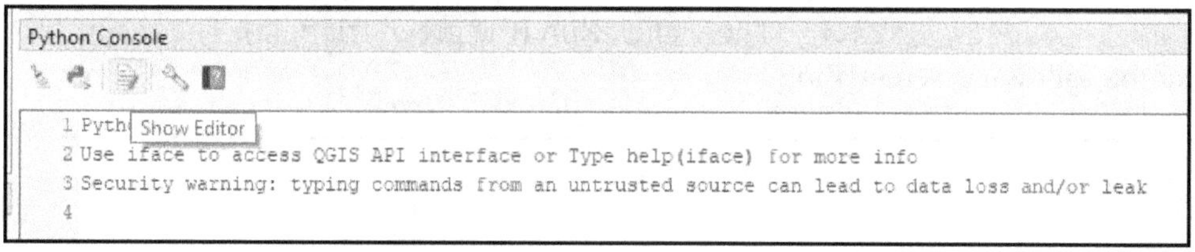

The Python Console

Copy the following code into the script editor:

```
Airport_layer =
iface.addVectorLayer('D:/QGIS_quickstart/qgis_sample_data/shapefiles/airpor
ts.shp','airports','ogr')

Alaska_layer =
iface.addVectorLayer('D:/QGIS_quickstart/qgis_sample_data/shapefiles/alaska
.shp','alaska','ogr')

print (Airport_layer.name())

print (Airport_layer.featureCount())

## print the attribute table

airportFeatures = Airport_layer.getFeatures()

for feature in airportFeatures:
    print (feature.attributes())
```

Or, alternatively, you can download data from `https://github.com/PacktPublishing/`
`QGIS-Quick-Start-Guide/blob/master/Chapter07/01_Loading_Data.py`. Be sure to re
point to your data location. Click on the Save As button in the editor to save the file to your
project as `01_Loading_data.py`. Then, click Run (the green triangle). The result should
look like the following screenshot:

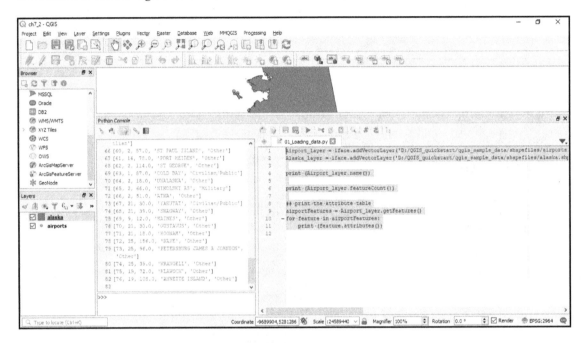

The script in the Python Console

To learn more about the vector class, have a look at the documentation here: `https://qgis.`
`org/api/classQgsVectorLayer.html`.

Loading raster data

Let's build another script to load raster data. Copy the following code:

```
Hillshade_layer =
iface.addRasterLayer('D:/QGIS_quickstart/qgis_sample_data/raster/SR_50M_ala
ska_nad.tif','Hillshade')

Landcover_layer =
iface.addRasterLayer('D:/QGIS_quickstart/qgis_sample_data/raster/landcover.
img','Landcover')
```

```
## print the layer names

print (Hillshade_layer.name())

print (Landcover_layer.name())

## print the image dimensions

print (Hillshade_layer.width(), Hillshade_layer.height())

print (Landcover_layer.width(), Landcover_layer.height())
```

The code in this script is loading in two layers, `Hillshade` and `Landcover`, printing the names to the console, and printing the image dimensions.

You can download data from here: https://github.com/PacktPublishing/QGIS-Quick-Start-Guide/blob/master/Chapter07/02_Loading_data_raster.py. Be sure to repoint to your data location if different to the script. Click on the Save As button in the editor to save the file to your project as `02_Loading_data_raster.py`. Then, click Run (the green triangle). The result should look like the following screenshot:

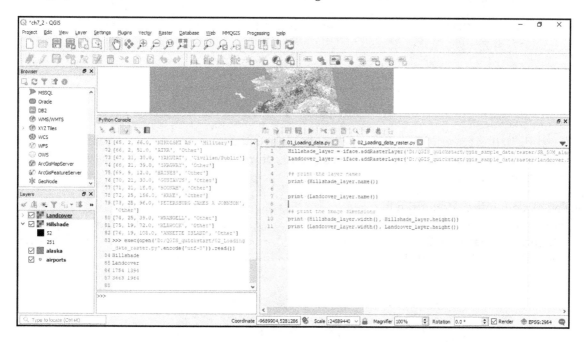

The script in the Python Console

To explore more about the `Raster` class, have a look at the documentation here: `https://qgis.org/api/classQgsRasterLayer.html`.

We can write scripts to automate many processes in QGIS from rendering, map creation, and processing. In fact, all parts of this book could be automated. Let's finish this section on Python and scripting with one last spatial processing script. This time, we will buffer the `airports` layers.

Buffer script

Open a new project in QGIS. Copy the following code to the editor:

```
## Buffering

Airport_layer =
iface.addVectorLayer('D:/QGIS_quickstart/qgis_sample_data/shapefiles/airpor
ts.shp','airports','ogr')

param = { 'INPUT' : Airport_layer, 'DISTANCE' : 15000, 'SEGMENTS' : 5,
'END_CAP_STYLE' : 0, 'JOIN_STYLE' : 0, 'MITER_LIMIT' : 2, 'DISSOLVE' :
False, 'OUTPUT' : 'memory:' }

algoOutput = processing.run("qgis:buffer", param)

Airport_buffer = QgsProject.instance().addMapLayer(algoOutput['OUTPUT'])
```

The code in this script loads the `airports` layer, sets the buffering parameters (`param`), calls the `qgis` buffer with the `processing.run` command, and then adds a layer called `OUTPUT` to the map.

You can download data from here: `https://github.com/PacktPublishing/QGIS-Quick-Start-Guide/blob/master/Chapter07/03_Buffer_Airport.py`. Be sure to repoint to your data location. Save the file to your project as `03_Buffer_airport.py`. Then, click Run (the green triangle). The result should look like the following screenshot:

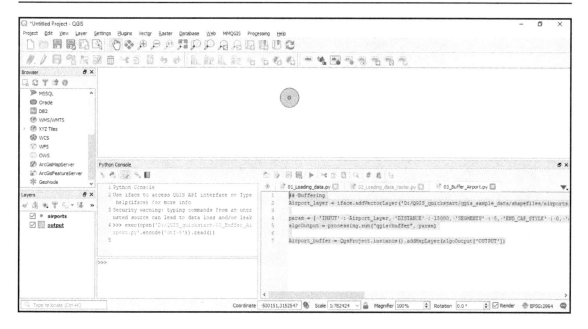

The script in the Python Console

If you wish to learn more about programming with Python in QGIS, this is a good resource with plenty of script examples: https://docs.qgis.org/testing/pdf/en/QGIS-testing-PyQGISDeveloperCookbook-en.pdf.

Summary

In this final chapter, we have looked at extending QGIS. We looked at three options: building models using the model builder, accessing plugins, and the Python Console. The ability to extend QGIS is perhaps the most convincing reason to use the software. You can customize it to your needs, you can download plugins that others have written, and you can automate the boring repetitive stuff. Models, scripts, and Plugins are all shareable.

Other Books You May Enjoy

If you enjoyed this book, you may be interested in these other books by Packt:

Learn QGIS - Fourth Edition
Andrew Cutts, Anita Graser

ISBN: 9781788997423

- Explore various ways to load data into QGIS
- Understand how to style data and present it in a map
- Create maps and explore ways to expand them
- Get acquainted with the new processing toolbox in QGIS 3.4
- Manipulate your geospatial data and gain quality insights
- Understand how to customize QGIS 3.4
- Work with QGIS 3.4 in 3D

Hands-On Geospatial Analysis with R and QGIS
Shammunul Islam

ISBN: 9781788991674

- Install R and QGIS
- Get familiar with the basics of R programming and QGIS
- Visualize quantitative and qualitative data to create maps
- Find out the basics of raster data and how to use them in R and QGIS
- Perform geoprocessing tasks and automate them using the graphical modeler of QGIS
- Apply different machine learning algorithms on satellite data for landslide susceptibility mapping and prediction

Leave a review - let other readers know what you think

Please share your thoughts on this book with others by leaving a review on the site that you bought it from. If you purchased the book from Amazon, please leave us an honest review on this book's Amazon page. This is vital so that other potential readers can see and use your unbiased opinion to make purchasing decisions, we can understand what our customers think about our products, and our authors can see your feedback on the title that they have worked with Packt to create. It will only take a few minutes of your time, but is valuable to other potential customers, our authors, and Packt. Thank you!

Index

about 102, 103
regions intersect pipelines 103, 104, 106, 107
used, for tracing building within 500 m of pipeline
   107, 109, 111
used, for tracing landcover types in buffered
   pipeline 111, 113
used, for tracing settlements within 500 m of
   pipeline 107, 109, 111
Python command line
   layer, inspecting 141, 142
   scripts, building on 142, 144
   scripts, building to buffer airports layers 146,
      147
   scripts, building to load raster data 144, 146
   using 139
   vector layer, loading 140

Q

QGIS project
   creating 25
   saving 38
QGIS, projection
   data, saving 35, 37, 38
QGIS, Semi-Automatic Classification Plugin
   reference 138
QGIS
   downloading link 6
   installing 6
   installing, on Ubuntu 12, 13
   installing, on Windows 6
   map navigation toolbar 16, 17
   map, creating 89, 92, 94
   panel and toolbar, customizing 14, 15
   panel overview 13
   panels 14
   plugins 131
   projections 32, 34, 35
   toolbar overview 13
   toolbars 14, 16, 17
   using 13
Query Builder
   about 73, 75
   used, to build query 73, 75

query
   building, with Query Builder 73, 75

R

raster analysis 113, 114, 117, 119
raster data
   combining, with vector data 111
   converting, to vector data 120, 122, 123
   creating 56
   styling 75, 78
raster dataset
   creating 56, 57
Raster Toolbar 79
regions intersect pipelines 103, 104, 106, 107
rivers layer
   line data, styling 68

S

scratch layers
   about 53, 54
   data, saving to shapefiles 55
Semi-Automatic Classification Plugin (SCP) 132,
   135, 138
styles
   saving 79, 81

U

Ubuntu
   QGIS, installing on 12, 13
Upper Left (UL) 135

V

vector data
   line data, styling 68
   points, styling 69, 73
   polygon data, styling 61, 64, 67
   styling 61

W

web map
   creating 98, 99
Windows
   QGIS, installing on 6

CPSIA information can be obtained
at www.ICGtesting.com
Printed in the USA
LVHW061346141122
733086LV00011B/493